Dream Athens: A Travel Preparation Guide.

Daniel Hunter

TABLE OF CONTENTS

Introduction

Welcome to Athens, a city that has stood as a symbol of human achievement and ingenuity for thousands of years. As you embark on your journey to this historic metropolis, you are not merely embarking on a vacation; you are embarking on a voyage through time. Athens, the capital of Greece, is a living museum of world history, a place where the ancient and the modern coexist in a seamless blend of culture, cuisine, and charm.

Known as the "Cradle of Civilization," Athens boasts a legacy that stretches back over 3,400 years. It was here that democracy was born, where great philosophers like Socrates and Aristotle pondered the mysteries of the universe, and where artists and architects created timeless masterpieces. But Athens is not stuck in the past; it is a vibrant, dynamic city that continues to evolve, offering visitors a rich tapestry of experiences.

In this Athens Travel Guide, we will be your compass through this remarkable city. Whether you are a history enthusiast, an adventurer seeking the thrill of exploration, a food lover eager to savor Mediterranean flavors, or simply a traveler in search of unforgettable memories, Athens has something special for you.

Athens is a city that caters to all types of travelers, from solo wanderers seeking self-discovery to families creating lasting memories together. So, whether you're standing atop the Acropolis, gazing at the Parthenon, or sipping Greek coffee in a quaint café, remember that Athens is a city where history is not just studied in books but is alive in the stones and stories of its streets. We invite you to open your heart and mind to the magic of Athens, where every step you take is a journey through time, and every moment is an opportunity to connect with the essence of human civilization.

As you turn the pages of this guide, allow yourself to be captivated by Athens, where the past meets the present in an unforgettable embrace. Your Athenian adventure awaits.

Chapter 1. Athens

- Overview of Athens as a Travel Destination

Welcome to Athens, the cradle of Western civilization and a city where history and modernity coexist harmoniously. Nestled in the heart of Greece, Athens is a captivating destination that seamlessly blends ancient wonders with a vibrant contemporary scene. Whether you're a history enthusiast, a food lover, an art aficionado, or a traveler seeking a unique cultural experience, Athens has something to offer every type of visitor. Here's an overview of what makes Athens a must-visit destination:

Historical Significance:
Athens is a city that breathes history. It's the birthplace of democracy, philosophy, and theater, and its historical importance is palpable as you walk through its ancient streets. The Acropolis, crowned by the iconic Parthenon, stands as a symbol of the city's rich past and is a UNESCO World Heritage site. The Acropolis Museum, National Archaeological Museum, and numerous archaeological sites reveal the city's ancient treasures.

Architectural Marvels:
The juxtaposition of ancient and modern architecture in Athens is truly remarkable. While the Acropolis steals the show, the city is also adorned with neoclassical buildings, Byzantine churches, and Ottoman-era monuments. The Plaka neighborhood, with its labyrinthine streets and neoclassical facades, offers a glimpse into old Athens, while the modernist designs of structures like the Stavros Niarchos Foundation Cultural Center showcase the city's contemporary side.

Cultural Vibrancy:
Athens boasts a thriving cultural scene that spans from classical music concerts to contemporary art exhibitions. The Odeon of Herodes Atticus, an ancient amphitheater nestled beneath the Acropolis, hosts concerts and performances, creating a unique backdrop for cultural events. The city's galleries, theaters, and music venues offer a diverse array of artistic experiences for travelers seeking to immerse themselves in Greek culture.

Gastronomic Delights:
Greek cuisine is celebrated worldwide, and Athens is the perfect place to savor its authentic flavors. From bustling street markets to traditional tavernas, you can indulge in mouthwatering dishes

like souvlaki, moussaka, and baklava. Don't forget to pair your meal with a glass of ouzo or retsina. For foodies, Athens is a paradise of tastes and aromas.

Mediterranean Lifestyle:
Athens embodies the relaxed Mediterranean way of life. Enjoy leisurely strolls through the charming neighborhoods, sip coffee at sidewalk cafes while people-watching, and embrace the "philoxenia" (hospitality) of the locals. The warm, sunny climate adds to the city's allure, making it a year-round destination.

Gateway to Greek Islands:
Athens also serves as a convenient gateway to the idyllic Greek islands. From the bustling port of Piraeus, you can embark on island-hopping adventures to destinations like Santorini, Mykonos, and Crete. The Greek islands offer a contrasting experience to Athens, with their pristine beaches, turquoise waters, and charming villages.

Athens, with its deep historical roots, vibrant culture, and warm hospitality, is a city that leaves a lasting impression on every traveler. Whether you're exploring ancient ruins, savoring delectable cuisine, or simply basking in the Mediterranean sun, Athens offers a diverse range of experiences that will make your visit unforgettable. So, pack your bags and get ready to embark on a journey through time and tradition in this captivating city. Athens awaits, promising you an adventure like no other.

- Brief History and Cultural Significance

Athens, the capital of Greece, is a city steeped in history that stretches back over 3,400 years. Its story begins in the Bronze Age when it was a small settlement atop the Acropolis hill. However, it rose to prominence during the Classical period (5th and 4th centuries BCE) as the epicenter of ancient Greek civilization.

1. The Golden Age of Athens: Athens' zenith came under the rule of Pericles when it became a center of culture, philosophy, art, and democracy. This era saw the construction of iconic monuments such as the Parthenon and the development of radical ideas by philosophers like Socrates, Plato, and Aristotle.

2. The Peloponnesian War: Athens' power led to conflict with Sparta, resulting in the devastating Peloponnesian War (431-404 BCE). While Athens eventually fell, its legacy endured.

3. Roman and Byzantine Periods: Athens became part of the Roman Empire in the 2nd century BCE and later the Byzantine Empire. During this time, it remained an important city but experienced a decline in political significance.

4. Ottoman Rule: Athens was under Ottoman rule from the late 15th century until the Greek War of Independence in the early 19th century. This period saw the city's transformation into a provincial Ottoman town.

5. Modern Greece: Athens became the capital of Greece in 1834 following the country's independence. It underwent rapid development, especially in the late 19th and early 20th centuries.

Cultural Significance:

Athens holds immense cultural significance, both historically and in the contemporary world.

1. Birthplace of Democracy: Athens is celebrated as the birthplace of democracy. The Athenian system of government, developed in the 5th century BCE, laid the foundation for modern democratic systems around the world.

2. Philosophy and Education: The city produced some of history's greatest philosophers, including Socrates, Plato, and Aristotle. Their ideas continue to shape Western philosophy and education.

3. The Arts: Athens has long been a cultural hub. During the Golden Age, it was the center of Greek drama and the birthplace of theater, with playwrights like Aeschylus, Sophocles, and Euripides. Today, the city is home to numerous theaters, museums, and art galleries.

4. Architecture: The architectural marvels of ancient Athens, including the Parthenon, remain iconic symbols of classical architecture and continue to inspire architects worldwide.

5. Olympic Heritage: Athens hosted the first modern Olympic Games in 1896, reviving the ancient tradition. This event marked the beginning of the modern Olympic movement.

6. Culinary Heritage: Greek cuisine, with its delicious offerings like moussaka, souvlaki, and baklava, is celebrated globally. In Athens, you can savor both traditional and contemporary Greek dishes.

7. Contemporary Culture: Athens is a dynamic, modern city with a thriving arts scene, nightlife, and a rich contemporary culture. Its blend of ancient history and modern vitality makes it a unique and captivating destination.

In summary, Athens is not only a city of historical significance but also a cultural treasure trove that continues to influence the world. Its ancient heritage and modern vibrancy make it a must-visit destination for travelers seeking a rich and multifaceted experience.

- *Weather and Best Times to Visit*

Athens, the ancient and vibrant capital of Greece, offers a rich blend of history, culture, and contemporary life. When planning your trip to this remarkable city, it's crucial to consider the weather and the best times to visit to make the most of your experience.

Weather Overview:
Athens enjoys a Mediterranean climate, characterized by hot, dry summers and mild, wet winters. Here's a breakdown of the seasons:

1. Spring (March to May): Spring is an ideal time to visit Athens. The weather is pleasantly warm, and

the city is covered in a colorful tapestry of blooming flowers. Expect temperatures ranging from 15°C to 25°C (59°F to 77°F). It's a great time for outdoor exploration without the scorching summer heat.

2. Summer (June to August): Summers in Athens are hot and dry, with temperatures often exceeding 30°C (86°F). This is the peak tourist season, with visitors flocking to see the ancient ruins and enjoy the Mediterranean beaches. Be prepared for crowded attractions and higher prices, but the lively atmosphere is infectious.

3. Autumn (September to November): Early autumn is a pleasant time to visit, with warm days and cooler nights. September is particularly lovely, and it's still possible to enjoy outdoor activities. Temperatures range from 18°C to 28°C (64°F to 82°F). As autumn progresses, the weather cools down, making it comfortable for exploring the city's historical sites.

4. Winter (December to February): Athens experiences a mild winter compared to many other European cities, but it can be quite rainy. Daytime temperatures hover around 12°C to 16°C (54°F to 61°F). While it's not the best time for beach activities, it's an excellent opportunity to explore

museums, cozy cafes, and the city's cultural scene without the crowds.

Best Times to Visit:

1. Spring (March to May): This is the optimal time to visit Athens. The weather is delightful for outdoor activities, and you'll experience the city's beauty without the intense summer crowds.

2. Early Autumn (September): If you want to avoid the peak summer tourist rush but still enjoy pleasant weather, September is a fantastic choice. The sea is warm for swimming, and the evenings are comfortably cool.

3. Late Autumn (October to November): For a quieter and more affordable trip, late autumn is ideal. The weather remains pleasant for sightseeing, and you can catch the city's cultural events without the summer crowds.

4. Winter (December to February): If you prefer a more local experience and are interested in indoor attractions like museums and historic sites, consider visiting Athens in the winter. Hotel rates are lower, and you'll find fewer tourists.

In conclusion, the best time to visit Athens largely depends on your preferences and interests. Whether you're drawn to the lively summer atmosphere or the peaceful ambiance of the off-peak seasons, Athens welcomes you year-round with its rich history, culture, and warm Mediterranean spirit.

Chapter 2. Essential Travel Planning

- *Visa Requirements and Entry Information*

Before embarking on your journey to Athens, Greece, it's essential to be aware of the visa requirements and entry information to ensure a smooth and hassle-free entry into this captivating city. here's what you need to know:

1. Visa Requirements:

   a. Schengen Visa: Greece is part of the Schengen Area, which allows travelers from certain countries to enter Athens and the rest of Greece without a visa for short stays of up to 90 days within a 180-day period. If you are a citizen of a Schengen member country or a visa-exempt country, you typically won't need a visa for tourism or business purposes.

   b. Visa-Required Countries: If you are not from a Schengen member country or a visa-exempt country, you will need to apply for a Schengen Visa at the Greek consulate or embassy in your home country before traveling to Athens.

c. Long-Term Stay: If you plan to stay in Athens for longer than 90 days for work, study, or other purposes, you will need to apply for a Greek National Visa or Residence Permit. The requirements for these visas can vary depending on your specific situation, so it's best to check with the Greek consulate or embassy in your country.

2. Passport Requirements:

Make sure your passport is valid for at least three months beyond your planned departure from Athens. It's also a good practice to have at least two blank pages in your passport for entry and exit stamps.

3. Entry Information:

a. Entry Points: Most international travelers to Athens arrive at Eleftherios Venizelos International Airport (ATH), which is well-connected to the city center by various transportation options. Other entry points include the ports of Piraeus and Patras if you are arriving by ferry.

b. Customs Regulations: Greece has specific customs regulations, and it's essential to be aware of what you can and cannot bring into the country.

Ensure you declare any items of value or special interest when entering Greece.

   c. Currency: The currency in Athens is the Euro (€). You can exchange currency at the airport, banks, or ATMs throughout the city.

   d. Language: The official language is Greek, but English is widely spoken in tourist areas.

   e. Health and Safety: Make sure you have travel insurance that covers health emergencies, as well as any necessary vaccinations or health precautions recommended for your trip.

   f. Local Laws and Customs: Familiarize yourself with the local laws and customs in Athens to ensure a respectful and enjoyable visit.

Please note that visa and entry requirements can change, so it's essential to verify the most up-to-date information with the Greek consulate or embassy in your country and stay informed about any changes in regulations or travel advisories. Safe travels and enjoy your time exploring the vibrant city of Athens!

- Currency, Payment Methods, and Budgeting Tips

When planning your trip to Athens, it's crucial to understand the currency, payment methods, and budgeting tips to make your stay in this historic city both convenient and cost-effective. Here's what you need to know:

Currency:

The official currency in Athens is the Euro (€). Greece adopted the Euro in 2001, making it easy for travelers to handle transactions without the need for currency exchange. You'll find banknotes and coins in various denominations, with coins ranging from 1 cent to 2 euros and banknotes from 5 to 500 euros.

Payment Methods:

1. Cash: While many places in Athens accept credit and debit cards, it's advisable to carry some cash, especially for small purchases, market stalls, and transportation. ATMs are widely available throughout the city, making it easy to withdraw Euros when needed.

2. Credit and Debit Cards: Major credit and debit cards, such as Visa and MasterCard, are widely accepted in hotels, restaurants, and larger stores. Be sure to inform your bank of your travel plans to avoid any card issues abroad.

3. Contactless Payments: Contactless payment methods, such as Apple Pay and Google Wallet, are becoming increasingly popular and can be used at various establishments.

4. Travel Cards: Consider using prepaid travel cards that allow you to load funds in Euros before your trip. These cards are secure and can be a useful budgeting tool.

Budgeting Tips:

1. Daily Budget: Athens offers a wide range of options for travelers with varying budgets. On average, you can expect to spend between €100 to €150 per day per person. This budget includes meals, transportation, and some sightseeing.

2. Eating Out: Dining at local tavernas and street food vendors can be cost-effective while providing a taste of authentic Greek cuisine. Look for daily

specials or "menu of the day" deals for even better value.

3. Transportation: Utilize public transportation, including buses and the Athens Metro, which is efficient and budget-friendly. Consider purchasing multi-day transportation passes for extra savings.

4. Entrance Fees: Many of Athens' historical sites and museums have entrance fees. Plan your visits strategically and consider purchasing combination tickets if you intend to visit multiple attractions.

5. Shopping: Athens offers excellent shopping opportunities, from flea markets to luxury boutiques. Set a shopping budget and try bargaining at markets for unique souvenirs.

6. Tipping: Tipping is customary in Athens, with 10% to 15% of the bill as a standard tip at restaurants. It's also common to round up taxi fares.

7. Free Attractions: Take advantage of free attractions like the Acropolis Hill, where you can enjoy panoramic views of the city without paying an entrance fee.

By understanding the currency, payment methods, and these budgeting tips, you can make the most of your Athens experience while staying within your financial comfort zone. Athens offers a rich cultural experience without breaking the bank, allowing you to immerse yourself in its history and vibrant atmosphere.

- Health and Safety Considerations

Ensuring your health and safety is a top priority when visiting Athens, Greece. Here are essential health and safety considerations to keep in mind for a worry-free trip:

1. Medical Care:
   - Athens boasts a well-developed healthcare system with modern hospitals and clinics. In case of emergencies, dial 112 for immediate assistance.
   - Make sure your travel insurance covers medical emergencies and evacuation if necessary.
   - Carry any prescription medications you may need, along with a copy of your prescription.

2. Vaccinations:
   - Check with your healthcare provider for recommended vaccinations before traveling to Greece. Routine vaccines should be up to date.

- Hepatitis A and B vaccines may be advisable, depending on your travel plans.

3. Safety Precautions:
  - Athens is generally a safe city for tourists, but like any major urban area, it's essential to stay vigilant.
  - Be cautious of pickpocketing, especially in crowded areas like public transportation and tourist sites.
  - Keep your belongings secure and avoid displaying expensive items.
  - Use well-lit and populated streets at night, and be aware of your surroundings.

4. Water and Food Safety:
  - Tap water in Athens is typically safe to drink, but some people may prefer bottled water.
  - Greek cuisine is delightful, but exercise caution with street food vendors. Opt for established restaurants to minimize the risk of foodborne illnesses.

5. Traffic and Transportation:
  - Be cautious when crossing streets, as traffic in Athens can be chaotic. Use designated crosswalks and obey traffic signals.

- Public transportation, including the metro, trams, and buses, is a convenient and safe way to get around the city.

6. Emergency Contacts:
  - Emergency services: 112 (medical, fire, police)
  - Tourist Police: 171 (for non-urgent assistance and reporting incidents involving tourists)
  - Embassy or Consulate: Know the location and contact information of your country's embassy or consulate in Athens.

7. Natural Disasters:
  - Athens is not prone to natural disasters like earthquakes or hurricanes, but it's wise to be informed about the local emergency procedures and evacuation routes.

By following these health and safety considerations, you can enjoy your visit to Athens with peace of mind, focusing on exploring its rich history, culture, and breathtaking sights. Always stay informed about current conditions and adapt your plans accordingly for a safe and memorable trip.

- *Local Etiquette and Cultural Insights*

To fully appreciate your visit to Athens, it's important to understand and respect the local etiquette and cultural norms. Here are some insights to help you navigate Athens' vibrant culture:

1. Greetings and Politeness:
   - Greeks are known for their warm hospitality. When meeting someone, a friendly handshake and a warm smile are customary.
   - It's common to address people using their titles and last names, especially in formal settings. However, among friends and in casual situations, first names are often used.

2. Punctuality:
   - While punctuality is valued in business and formal settings, social gatherings tend to start a bit later than the appointed time. Arriving fashionably late, around 15 to 30 minutes, is generally acceptable.

3. Respect for Traditions:
   - Greece has a rich history and cultural traditions. When visiting churches or monasteries, dress modestly, covering shoulders and knees. Silence and respect are expected in these sacred places.
   - When participating in traditional Greek events or celebrations, such as weddings or festivals, embrace the customs and traditions. Dancing the

traditional Syrtaki dance, for example, is a joyful way to immerse yourself in Greek culture.

4. Dining Etiquette:
   - When dining in a Greek home, it's customary to bring a small gift for the host, such as wine, dessert, or flowers.
   - Wait for the host or hostess to start the meal before you begin eating. Greeks often share dishes family-style.
   - Tipping is customary in restaurants and cafes. A tip of 10-15% is appreciated.

5. Gesture and Body Language:
   - Greeks are expressive and may use hand gestures to emphasize their speech. Gestures like the "Moutza" (an open hand with fingers spread) are considered offensive, so it's best to avoid using unfamiliar gestures.
   - Pointing at people is considered impolite. Instead, gesture with an open hand.

6. Hospitality and Offerings:
   - Greeks are known for their hospitality. If invited into a Greek home, expect to be offered coffee, sweets, or even a meal. Accepting these offerings is a sign of respect and friendship.

7. Language:
   - While Greek is the official language, English is widely spoken in tourist areas. Learning a few basic Greek phrases, such as "hello" (Yasou) and "thank you" (Efharisto), can be appreciated by locals.

8. Respect for Monuments and Historical Sites:
   - Athens is home to numerous historical and archaeological treasures. When visiting ancient sites like the Acropolis, follow all posted rules and guidelines. Climbing on or touching ancient monuments is generally prohibited to preserve these cultural treasures.

By embracing these local etiquette and cultural insights, you'll not only show respect for Athens' rich heritage but also enhance your travel experience by connecting with the warm and welcoming people of this iconic city. Enjoy your time exploring Athens!

Chapter 3. Getting to Know Athens

- *Orientation to the City's Neighborhoods*

Athens, the vibrant capital of Greece, is a city steeped in history and brimming with diverse neighborhoods, each offering a unique atmosphere and experiences. To make the most of your visit, it's essential to get acquainted with the various neighborhoods that compose this captivating metropolis:

1. Plaka: Often referred to as the "Neighborhood of the Gods," Plaka is nestled at the foot of the Acropolis. This picturesque district is known for its charming, narrow streets, neoclassical architecture, and an abundance of cafes, restaurants, and boutiques. It's a perfect place to start your journey and immerse yourself in Athens' ancient charm.

2. Monastiraki: Adjacent to Plaka, Monastiraki is a bustling area famous for its flea market. Here, you can explore an array of antique shops, quirky boutiques, and enjoy the local street food scene. Don't forget to visit the Monastiraki Square and the iconic Tzistarakis Mosque.

3. Syntagma: The heart of Athens, Syntagma Square, is surrounded by neoclassical buildings,

luxury hotels, and the Greek Parliament. Witness the Changing of the Guard ceremony at the Tomb of the Unknown Soldier and stroll through the National Garden, an oasis of greenery in the city center.

4. Kolonaki: This upscale neighborhood is synonymous with luxury shopping, fine dining, and a cosmopolitan ambiance. Kolonaki is also home to the Benaki Museum and the Museum of Cycladic Art.

5. Exarchia: Known for its bohemian spirit, Exarchia is a hub for artists and intellectuals. The neighborhood boasts street art, alternative bars, and a youthful energy. It's a unique enclave in the heart of Athens.

6. Gazi: Once an industrial area, Gazi has transformed into Athens' nightlife epicenter. The former gasworks buildings now house trendy bars, nightclubs, and restaurants. It's the place to experience Athens' contemporary nightlife scene.

7. Psiri: A historic district just north of Monastiraki, Psiri is a maze of narrow streets filled with traditional tavernas, live music venues, and a lively

atmosphere. It's the perfect spot for an authentic Greek meal and entertainment.

8. Exarchia: Known for its bohemian spirit, Exarchia is a hub for artists and intellectuals. The neighborhood boasts street art, alternative bars, and a youthful energy. It's a unique enclave in the heart of Athens.

9. Kerameikos: This neighborhood is named after the ancient cemetery and the archaeological site of Kerameikos. It's a quieter area, ideal for exploring ancient ruins and enjoying a peaceful stroll along the Kerameikos Cemetery.

10. Kifisia: Located in the northern suburbs, Kifisia is an affluent neighborhood known for its upscale shopping, beautiful parks, and elegant villas. It offers a tranquil escape from the city center.

As you explore Athens, you'll discover that each neighborhood contributes to the city's rich tapestry of culture, history, and modernity. Whether you're seeking ancient wonders, contemporary art, vibrant nightlife, or peaceful retreats, Athens' diverse neighborhoods have something to offer every traveler.

- *Public Transportation Options (Metro, Buses, Trams)*

Athens, the historic capital of Greece, offers a comprehensive public transportation system that makes exploring the city and its many attractions convenient and affordable. Here's an overview of the primary modes of public transportation in Athens:

1. Athens Metro:
   - The Athens Metro is one of the most efficient ways to navigate the city. It consists of three lines: Line 1 (green), Line 2 (red), and Line 3 (blue). These lines connect key areas of Athens, including the city center, suburbs, and major attractions.
   - The metro is clean, safe, and known for its punctuality. It's a popular choice for tourists, especially when visiting landmarks like the Acropolis, Syntagma Square, and Monastiraki.

2. Buses:
   - Athens has an extensive bus network that covers virtually every corner of the city, making it a flexible option for getting around. Bus routes are well-marked, and the vehicles are air-conditioned.
   - Several bus lines run 24/7, providing transportation during both day and night. They

serve not only the city center but also the suburbs and coastal areas.

3. Trams:
  - The Athens Tram Network is another excellent way to explore the city, especially the coastal neighborhoods like Glyfada and Piraeus. The tram offers scenic views of the Athens Riviera and the Saronic Gulf.
  - Trams run from early morning until late at night, and tickets can be purchased at stations or on board.

4. Trolleybuses:
  - Trolleybuses are electric buses that run on overhead wires. They operate on several routes, and like regular buses, they provide an additional means of public transportation in Athens.

5. Integrated Ticketing:
  - Athens offers an integrated ticketing system, allowing passengers to use multiple modes of public transportation with a single ticket. You can purchase various types of tickets, including single-ride tickets, daily passes, and multi-day cards.
  - The Athens Transport Ticket is valid for the metro, buses, trams, and trolleybuses, making it a

cost-effective choice for tourists planning to explore the city extensively.

6. Athens Public Transport App:
   - To make using public transportation even more convenient, consider downloading the Athens Public Transport app. It provides real-time information on schedules, routes, and ticket purchasing options.

7. Accessibility:
   - Athens' public transportation system is accessible to people with disabilities. Many metro stations have elevators, ramps, and tactile paving, and buses are equipped to accommodate passengers with special needs.

Navigating Athens using its public transportation system is not only practical but also an excellent way to experience the local way of life. Whether you're headed to ancient archaeological sites, vibrant neighborhoods, or scenic coastal areas, Athens' public transportation options have you covered, making your visit to this historic city both enjoyable and convenient.

- *Renting Cars and Bikes: Pros and Cons*

Exploring Athens, Greece, can be an exciting adventure, and one of the key decisions you'll need to make is how to get around the city. Renting cars and bikes are popular options, each with its own set of advantages and disadvantages. Here's a breakdown to help you decide:

Renting Cars:

Pros:

1. Convenience: Having a rental car provides you with the flexibility to explore Athens and its surrounding areas at your own pace. You won't be tied to public transportation schedules.

2. Access to Outskirts: Athens boasts numerous attractions outside the city center, such as Cape Sounion and the Athenian Riviera. A car allows you to easily access these destinations.

3. Comfort: It's more comfortable, especially if you're traveling with a group or have a lot of luggage.

4. Air Conditioning: Athens can get scorching in the summer. Renting a car with air conditioning can make your journeys more comfortable.

Cons:

1. Traffic and Parking: Athens is known for its congested traffic and limited parking spaces. Finding parking, especially in the city center, can be challenging and costly.

2. Costs: Rental cars, fuel, and parking fees can add up quickly. Additionally, you may encounter tolls on highways.

3. Narrow Streets: Some areas of Athens have narrow and winding streets, which can be challenging to navigate, especially for larger vehicles.

4. Environmental Impact: If you're environmentally conscious, consider the impact of car emissions on the city's air quality.

Renting Bikes:

Pros:

1. Eco-Friendly: Biking is an eco-friendly mode of transportation that reduces your carbon footprint.

2. Easy Parking: Bicycles are easy to park and maneuver through Athens' narrow streets.

3. Healthy Lifestyle: It's a great way to stay active and explore the city at a leisurely pace.

4. Cost-Effective: Renting a bike is usually more affordable than renting a car, and you won't have to worry about fuel or parking fees.

Cons:

1. Limited Range: Biking is best suited for exploring the city center. It might not be as convenient for reaching attractions in the outskirts.

2. Traffic Risks: Athens' traffic can be chaotic, and some drivers may not be accustomed to sharing the road with cyclists. Be cautious and follow traffic rules.

3. Weather Dependency: Weather conditions, especially in the summer, can be hot and humid. Be prepared for the elements.

4. Physical Stamina: Biking requires a reasonable level of physical fitness. If you're not used to it, long rides might be tiring.

In conclusion, the choice between renting a car or a bike in Athens depends on your preferences, itinerary, and comfort level. For urban exploration and short distances within Athens, renting a bike can be an enjoyable and environmentally friendly option. On the other hand, if you plan to venture outside the city or prioritize comfort and convenience, a rental car might be more suitable. Consider your priorities and the pros and cons listed above to make the best choice for your Athens adventure.

- *Navigating Athens International Airport*

Arriving at Athens International Airport, also known as Eleftherios Venizelos International Airport (ATH), is often the first step in your Athens adventure. This modern and well-organized airport provides a welcoming entry point to the Greek capital. Here's a guide to help you navigate this bustling airport with ease:

1. Arrival Procedures:

- Immigration: After disembarking from your flight, proceed to the immigration counters for passport control. Ensure you have your valid passport and visa (if required) ready for inspection.

- Baggage Claim: Once through immigration, head to the baggage claim area to collect your luggage. Check the flight information screens for your baggage carousel assignment.

2. Customs and Security:

- Customs: After collecting your baggage, you will pass through customs. Be prepared to declare any items you may need to pay duties on or items of special interest.

- Security Check: Before leaving the baggage claim area, you may be subject to a security check. Follow the instructions of airport staff.

3. Ground Transportation:

- Taxis: If you prefer a taxi, the taxi rank is conveniently located just outside the arrivals hall. Licensed taxis are readily available and offer a convenient way to reach your destination in Athens.

- Public Transport: Athens International Airport is well-connected to the city center by public transportation. The Metro Line 3 (Blue Line) connects the airport to Syntagma Square in the city center. Buses and suburban railway options are also available.

- Car Rentals: If you plan to rent a car, several car rental companies have counters at the airport. You can pick up your vehicle at the designated car rental area just outside the arrivals hall.

4. Services and Amenities:

- Dining: The airport offers a range of dining options, from cafes and fast-food outlets to sit-down restaurants serving Greek and international cuisine.

- Shopping: Duty-free shops, boutiques, and souvenir stores are available if you'd like to do some shopping while at the airport.

- Lounges: If you have access to airport lounges through your airline or membership, there are several lounges within the airport where you can relax before your flight.

- Currency Exchange: Currency exchange counters and ATMs are located throughout the airport for your convenience.

5. Departures:

- Check-In: When departing Athens, check in for your flight at the airline's counters in the departures area. Many airlines also offer online check-in services.

- Security Check: After check-in, proceed to the security check area. Be prepared to remove your shoes, belts, and electronic devices for screening.

- Departure Gates: The airport has multiple departure gates, conveniently organized by terminal and gate number. Check your boarding pass for your departure gate information.

6. Accessibility:

- Athens International Airport is equipped with facilities to accommodate passengers with reduced mobility. Wheelchair assistance and accessible restrooms are available.

Navigating Athens International Airport is relatively straightforward, thanks to clear signage and helpful airport staff. Whether you're arriving in Athens for the first time or departing after a memorable visit, this airport ensures a comfortable and efficient travel experience, setting the stage for your exploration of this historic city.

Chapter 4. Accommodation Options

- *Luxury Hotels with Stunning Views*

Athens, the historic capital of Greece, is not only known for its ancient treasures but also for its luxurious accommodations offering breathtaking views of the city's iconic landmarks. If you're seeking a lavish stay with unforgettable vistas, here are some top luxury hotels to consider for your Athens visit:

1. Hotel Grande Bretagne, a Luxury Collection Hotel:
   - This historic hotel, located in the heart of Athens, offers opulent rooms and suites with panoramic views of the Acropolis and Syntagma Square.
   - Enjoy gourmet dining on the rooftop at the "GB Roof Garden Restaurant & Bar," where you can savor Mediterranean cuisine while gazing at the illuminated Acropolis.

2. King George, a Luxury Collection Hotel:
   - Adjacent to the Hotel Grande Bretagne, King George offers equally luxurious accommodations and fantastic Acropolis views.

- Their Tudor Hall Restaurant, with its neo-classical décor, provides an elegant setting for dining with a view of the Acropolis and the city.

3. Electra Metropolis Athens:
   - Situated near major historic sites, this modern luxury hotel boasts rooms and suites that overlook the Acropolis, Plaka, and Lycabettus Hill.
   - The rooftop "Metropolis Roof Garden" offers a stylish setting to enjoy a cocktail while taking in the mesmerizing cityscape.

4. New Hotel Athens:
   - This contemporary boutique hotel features uniquely designed rooms with artistic flair.
   - The rooftop "Art Lounge" presents a 360-degree view of Athens, including the Acropolis and the National Garden, making it an ideal spot for sunset drinks.

5. AthensWas Hotel:
   - Nestled in the historic district of Plaka, AthensWas offers modern luxury accommodations with private balconies and views of the Acropolis and the Acropolis Museum.
   - The rooftop "Sense Restaurant" allows you to savor Mediterranean cuisine while gazing at the Acropolis.

6. The Margi Hotel:
  - While not in the city center, The Margi offers a luxurious coastal escape in Vouliagmeni.
  - Some suites provide magnificent sea views, and you can unwind at the hotel's private beach or enjoy Mediterranean cuisine at "Nilaya Restaurant."

These luxury hotels not only pamper you with exquisite amenities and services but also provide you with the opportunity to wake up to or wind down with the mesmerizing views of Athens' historic and architectural marvels. Whether you're here for business or leisure, these hotels promise a truly enchanting stay in the heart of Greece's capital.

- Budget-Friendly Hostels and Guesthouses

For travelers seeking affordable accommodation in Athens without compromising comfort and convenience, the city offers a range of budget-friendly hostels and guesthouses. These options not only save you money but also provide opportunities to connect with fellow travelers and experience the local hospitality. Here are some excellent choices:

1. Athens Backpackers: Located in the heart of Plaka, Athens Backpackers is a popular hostel known for its vibrant atmosphere and social events. Dormitory-style rooms and private options are available. The rooftop bar offers fantastic views of the Acropolis.

2. Athenstyle: This hostel combines affordability with a fantastic location, just a stone's throw away from the Acropolis and Monastiraki Square. Athenstyle offers both dormitory beds and private rooms with en-suite bathrooms.

3. The Student and Travellers Inn: Situated near Syntagma Square, this cozy guesthouse provides affordable rooms with a friendly atmosphere. It's within walking distance of major attractions and public transportation hubs.

4. City Circus Athens: Set in a beautifully restored neoclassical building in the Psiri neighborhood, City Circus Athens offers dorms and private rooms. The artistic decor and rooftop terrace make it a unique and budget-friendly choice.

5. Fivos: Located near Omonia Square, Fivos is a budget-friendly guesthouse offering simple yet

comfortable rooms. It's a great base for exploring Athens on foot or by public transport.

6. Pella Inn Hostel: This hostel enjoys a prime location in Monastiraki, making it easy to explore the vibrant flea market and ancient ruins nearby. It offers dorms and private rooms with a friendly atmosphere.

7. Bedbox Hostel: Found in the Exarchia district, Bedbox Hostel is known for its affordability and eclectic design. It's a favorite among backpackers and budget-conscious travelers.

8. Athens Studios: Located near the Acropolis Museum, Athens Studios offers budget-friendly apartments, studios, and dormitories. The rooftop bar and swimming pool provide relaxation and stunning views.

9. Acropolis View Dream Hostel: As the name suggests, this hostel boasts incredible views of the Acropolis. It offers dormitory-style accommodation and is close to many attractions in the historic center.

10. Plaka Hotel: While not a traditional hostel, the Plaka Hotel offers budget-friendly rooms in the

charming Plaka neighborhood. It's a great option for those seeking comfort and affordability.

When booking any budget-friendly accommodation in Athens, consider factors such as location, reviews, and the amenities offered. Many of these hostels and guesthouses provide communal spaces, kitchen facilities, and organized tours to enhance your Athens experience. Keep in mind that prices and availability may vary, so it's advisable to book in advance, especially during peak tourist seasons. Enjoy your budget-friendly stay in Athens!

- Cozy Vacation Rentals and Airbnb Stays

When planning your visit to Athens, you'll find a plethora of accommodation options, but for those seeking a more personalized and homey experience, cozy vacation rentals and Airbnb stays are a fantastic choice. These options offer a unique opportunity to immerse yourself in the local culture while enjoying the comforts of home. Here's what you should know:

1. Airbnb in Athens:
   Airbnb has gained popularity in Athens, offering a wide range of accommodations, from quaint apartments to charming houses. Here's why you might consider booking an Airbnb stay:

- Local Experience: Staying in an Airbnb allows you to live like a local, often in residential neighborhoods where you can interact with Athenians and experience their daily life.

- Variety of Choices: You can find diverse listings that suit different budgets, preferences, and group sizes. Whether you want a cozy studio for a romantic getaway or a spacious villa for a family retreat, Athens has it all.

- Amenities: Many Airbnb properties come equipped with modern amenities like kitchens, Wi-Fi, and laundry facilities, providing added convenience during your stay.

2. Cozy Vacation Rentals:
   Athens also boasts a variety of cozy vacation rentals that can enhance your travel experience. These rentals are known for their homely atmosphere and personalized touches:

- Characterful Homes: Vacation rentals often reflect the unique character of Athens' architecture and design. You might find charming apartments in historic neighborhoods or traditional Greek cottages in the countryside.

- Local Hosts: Many vacation rentals are managed by local hosts who can offer valuable insights, recommendations, and a warm welcome. It's an excellent opportunity to connect with Athenians and gain insider knowledge about the city.

- Privacy and Comfort: Vacation rentals offer privacy and comfort, making them suitable for families, couples, or solo travelers who prefer a quieter and more relaxed environment.

3. Booking Tips:
- Plan Ahead: Since these accommodations can be in high demand, especially during peak tourist seasons, it's advisable to book well in advance to secure your preferred choice.

- Read Reviews: Take the time to read reviews from previous guests. They can provide valuable information about the property, the host, and the overall experience.

- Communication: Reach out to the host before booking to ask questions or clarify any doubts you may have. Good communication with the host can lead to a more pleasant stay.

4. Exploring Athens:

   Whether you choose an Airbnb or a vacation rental, Athens' key attractions, including the Acropolis, Plaka, and the National Archaeological Museum, are easily accessible. Public transportation options, such as the metro and buses, make it convenient to explore the city from your cozy base.

Booking a cozy vacation rental or an Airbnb stay in Athens allows you to enjoy the city at your own pace, relishing the comforts of a home away from home. It's a delightful way to make lasting memories in this historic and vibrant destination.

- Family-Friendly Accommodations and Services

Traveling with family to Athens is a fantastic experience, and the city offers a range of family-friendly accommodations and services to ensure a comfortable and enjoyable stay for visitors of all ages. Here are some options and services you can consider:

1. Family-Friendly Hotels: Athens boasts numerous hotels that cater specifically to families. These hotels often offer spacious family rooms or suites, children's play areas, and amenities like swimming

pools to keep the kids entertained. Some popular family-friendly hotel options include the Athens Marriott Hotel, Wyndham Grand Athens, and the Hilton Athens.

2. Vacation Rentals: Another excellent option for families is renting a vacation apartment or house. This provides more space, kitchen facilities, and a homely atmosphere. Websites like Airbnb and Vrbo have a variety of family-friendly properties in Athens.

3. Children's Activities: Athens is not just about ancient ruins; it also offers various child-friendly attractions. Places like the Attica Zoological Park, National Garden of Athens, and the Athens Planetarium are great for family outings.

4. Childcare Services: If parents need some alone time to explore Athens, many hotels offer childcare services or can recommend reputable babysitters.

5. Family-Friendly Dining: Athens has numerous restaurants that welcome families with open arms. Look for eateries with kid's menus and high chairs. Greeks are known for their hospitality, so don't be surprised if restaurant staff go out of their way to make your family feel comfortable.

6. Public Transportation: Athens has an extensive public transportation system that includes buses, trams, and the metro. Most are family-friendly, and children under a certain age often ride for free or at a reduced fare.

7. Parks and Playgrounds: Athens has several parks and playgrounds where kids can burn off energy. One of the best is the National Garden, a green oasis in the heart of the city with walking paths, ponds, and a small zoo.

8. Museums: While Athens is rich in history, not all museums are suitable for young children. However, the Museum of Greek Children's Art is an excellent choice, as it features art created by kids.

9. Emergency Services: Familiarize yourself with emergency contact numbers and the location of the nearest medical facilities, just in case.

10. Cultural Experiences: Consider attending family-friendly cultural events or performances. The Greek National Opera often hosts family-oriented shows, and outdoor concerts in Athens can be enjoyable for all ages.

Remember that Greeks are generally warm and welcoming towards families, so don't hesitate to ask for assistance or recommendations while exploring Athens with your loved ones. With the right accommodations and services, your family can make lasting memories in this historically rich and vibrant city.

Chapter 5. Sightseeing and Landmarks

- *Acropolis and Parthenon: Iconic Symbols of Athens*

No visit to Athens would be complete without exploring the awe-inspiring Acropolis and its crown jewel, the Parthenon. These ancient architectural marvels stand as enduring symbols of Athens and Greece's rich history, culture, and influence on Western civilization.

The Acropolis:

Perched majestically on a rocky hill overlooking the city of Athens, the Acropolis is a UNESCO World Heritage Site and one of the most iconic landmarks in the world. The name "Acropolis" translates to "High City," and it's a fitting description of this elevated citadel. Here are some key aspects of the Acropolis:

- Historical Significance: The Acropolis dates back to the 5th century BC and served as the religious and cultural heart of ancient Athens. It was dedicated to the goddess Athena, the city's patron deity.

- Architectural Marvels: The Acropolis is home to several impressive structures, including the Parthenon, the Erechtheion, the Propylaea (the grand entrance), and the Odeon of Herodes Atticus, an ancient theater.

- The Parthenon: The Parthenon, arguably the most famous building on the Acropolis, is a Doric temple dedicated to Athena Parthenos, the city's patron goddess. Its architectural perfection and historical significance make it a must-see attraction.

The Parthenon:

The Parthenon, with its elegant columns and timeless design, is an architectural masterpiece. Here's what you need to know about this iconic temple:

- Architectural Beauty: The Parthenon is renowned for its classical Doric style, with 46 outer columns and 19 inner columns. It was constructed using Pentelic marble and adorned with intricate friezes, metopes, and pediments.

- Historical Legacy: Built in the 5th century BC, the Parthenon not only served as a temple but also housed a massive statue of Athena Parthenos, which was made of gold and ivory.

- Restoration and Preservation: Over the centuries, the Parthenon has undergone various changes and damage, including bombings during the Venetian siege in the 17th century. Efforts to restore and preserve this historic site have been ongoing, ensuring its continued existence for future generations.

Visiting Tips:

- Plan your visit early in the day to avoid crowds and the heat, especially during the summer months.

- Wear comfortable shoes, as the uneven terrain and steep paths on the Acropolis hill can be challenging to navigate.

- Consider hiring a knowledgeable guide to gain deeper insights into the history and significance of these ancient wonders.

The Acropolis and the Parthenon are not just architectural treasures; they are windows into the past, offering a glimpse into the intellectual and artistic achievements of ancient Greece. They stand as enduring symbols of Athens, reminding visitors of the city's rich heritage and its lasting influence on the world. Make sure to include a visit to these iconic landmarks in your Athens travel itinerary for an unforgettable experience.

- *Ancient Agora and Temple of Hephaestus*

When visiting Athens, no exploration of the city's cultural heritage is complete without a journey to the Ancient Agora and the awe-inspiring Temple of Hephaestus. These historical landmarks offer a captivating glimpse into Athens' rich history and its enduring reverence for the gods.

1. Ancient Agora:

   a. Historical Significance: The Ancient Agora served as the heart of ancient Athens, functioning as a bustling marketplace and the civic, social, and political center of the city. It was a place where citizens gathered to discuss matters of governance and philosophy, making it an essential part of Athenian democracy.

   b. Exploring the Ruins: Today, the Ancient Agora stands as a captivating archaeological site with well-preserved ruins. You can wander through the remnants of stoa (colonnaded walkways), temples, and the impressive Temple of Hephaestus. Don't miss the reconstructed Stoa of Attalos, a two-story building that now houses the Museum of the Ancient Agora, featuring intriguing artifacts from daily life in ancient Athens.

   c. Highlights: Key attractions within the Agora include the Temple of Hephaestus, the Bouleuterion (Council Chamber), and the Odeon of Agrippa, which once hosted musical performances.

2. Temple of Hephaestus:

   a. Architectural Marvel: Standing majestically within the Ancient Agora, the Temple of Hephaestus, also known as Hephaisteion or Hephaestus Temple, is a Doric masterpiece of ancient Greek architecture. Built in the 5th century BC, it is one of the best-preserved temples from antiquity.

   b. Dedication: This temple was dedicated to Hephaestus, the ancient Greek god of blacksmiths, metalworking, and craftsmanship. The meticulous construction reflects the importance of Hephaestus in the lives of Athenians as a protector of their craftsmen.

c. Stunning Details: Marvel at the temple's graceful columns, intricate friezes, and the overall symmetry of its design. The interior was once adorned with sculptures and statues, though these have largely been lost to time.

Visiting the Ancient Agora and the Temple of Hephaestus offers a profound connection to Athens' classical past. As you stroll among these hallowed grounds, you can almost hear the echoes of philosophical debates and political discussions that shaped the city and Western civilization. Whether you're an archaeology enthusiast, history buff, or simply a curious traveler, these sites are essential stops on your Athens journey, offering a profound connection to the city's classical past and a chance to witness the enduring beauty of ancient Greek architecture and culture.

- National Archaeological Museum: Greek History Unveiled

One of the crown jewels of Athens' cultural landscape is the National Archaeological Museum, a treasure trove that unravels the rich tapestry of Greek history. Located in the Exarchia neighborhood, this museum stands as a testament to Greece's profound influence on art, culture, and civilization.

Highlights:

1. The Collection: The museum houses an astonishing collection of artifacts, spanning millennia of Greek history. Visitors can wander through halls filled with sculptures, pottery, jewelry, and more, all meticulously preserved. Notable exhibits include the Bronze Age Cycladic figurines, the awe-inspiring Antikythera Mechanism, and the mesmerizing Mask of Agamemnon.

2. Mythology and Legends: Greece's myths and legends come to life within these hallowed halls. Statues of gods and heroes, such as Zeus and Hercules, grace the museum, allowing you to connect with the stories that have shaped Western culture for centuries.

3. The Antikythera Mechanism: A true marvel of ancient engineering, this intricate device astounds visitors. Often referred to as the world's first computer, it's a testament to the Greeks' scientific and mathematical prowess.

4. Architectural Beauty: The museum's neoclassical architecture is an attraction in itself. With its grand

columns and elegant design, the building offers a fitting setting for the masterpieces within.

5. Temporary Exhibitions: The museum hosts temporary exhibitions that delve deeper into specific aspects of Greek history, art, and archaeology. These displays add fresh perspectives and ensure there's always something new to discover.

Practical Information:

- Location: 44 Patission Street, Exarchia, Athens.
- Opening Hours: The museum's opening hours can vary seasonally, so it's advisable to check the official website for the most up-to-date information.
- Admission: Entry fees apply, with reduced rates for students and seniors. Free admission is often available on specific days, such as Sundays during the winter months.

Tips for Visitors:

- Allocate ample time for your visit, as the museum's vast collection can be overwhelming.
- Consider hiring a guide or audio tour to gain a deeper understanding of the exhibits.

- Photography is allowed in most areas, but some sections may have restrictions, so pay attention to signage.
- The museum can get busy, especially during peak tourist seasons, so arriving early in the day can help you enjoy a quieter experience.

A visit to the National Archaeological Museum is a journey through Greece's remarkable past, providing invaluable insights into the foundations of Western civilization. Whether you're a history enthusiast, an art lover, or simply curious about the world's ancient wonders, this museum is an essential stop on your Athens adventure.

- Plaka District: Exploring Old Athens

When you step into the Plaka District in Athens, it's as if you've entered a time machine that transports you to the heart of old Athens. This charming and historic neighborhood, nestled beneath the slopes of the Acropolis, is a must-visit destination for travelers seeking a taste of Greece's rich history and vibrant culture. Here's what you can expect when exploring Plaka:

1. Timeless Architecture:

Plaka boasts a unique blend of neoclassical, Ottoman, and traditional Greek architecture. Wandering through its narrow, winding streets, you'll encounter whitewashed houses with colorful shutters, cobblestone pathways, and quaint squares. The district's authentic ambiance will make you feel like you've stepped back in time.

2. Acropolis Proximity:

One of Plaka's most significant advantages is its proximity to the Acropolis. You can easily walk to the ancient citadel from here, making it an ideal starting point for your Athens adventure. As you ascend towards the Acropolis, you'll pass several picturesque viewpoints offering stunning vistas of the city and the Parthenon.

3. Cultural Highlights:

Plaka is home to numerous museums, galleries, and cultural sites. Don't miss the Museum of Greek Folk Musical Instruments, which showcases an impressive collection of traditional musical instruments. Additionally, the Frissiras Museum, dedicated to contemporary European painting, is a hidden gem for art enthusiasts.

4. Shopping and Souvenirs:

The streets of Plaka are lined with quaint boutiques and souvenir shops. Here, you can shop for traditional Greek crafts, ceramics, jewelry, and locally-made products. Bargaining is not common in Athens, but you can still find unique items to bring home as mementos of your trip.

5. Authentic Greek Cuisine:

Plaka offers a diverse array of tavernas, restaurants, and cafes where you can savor authentic Greek cuisine. Try classic dishes like moussaka, souvlaki, or fresh seafood while enjoying outdoor dining in charming courtyards or under vine-covered pergolas.

6. Vibrant Nightlife:

As the sun sets, Plaka comes alive with a vibrant nightlife scene. You'll find lively bars and traditional Greek tavernas where you can enjoy live music, dance to Greek rhythms, and savor local wines or ouzo.

7. Historical Sites:

Within Plaka, you'll stumble upon historical sites such as the Roman Agora, the Tower of the Winds, and the Library of Hadrian. These ancient landmarks offer a glimpse into the city's rich past.

Whether you're interested in history, culture, shopping, or simply soaking in the atmosphere of a bygone era, Plaka District in Athens offers it all. It's a place where modern and ancient Greece gracefully coexist, making it an unmissable destination for any traveler exploring the captivating city of Athens.

- *Syntagma Square and Changing of the Guard Ceremony*

Syntagma Square, located in the heart of Athens, is not only a central transportation hub but also a vibrant civic space and a must-visit attraction for tourists. Here, you can immerse yourself in the city's rich history and culture and witness a captivating spectacle: the Changing of the Guard Ceremony.

Syntagma Square:

Syntagma Square, often referred to as Constitution Square, serves as the symbolic center of Athens. Surrounded by grand neoclassical buildings, it's a place where past and present seamlessly blend. Here's what you can expect when you visit:

- Hellenic Parliament: Dominating one side of the square is the Hellenic Parliament building. Its iconic facade and the honor guard in traditional Greek costume make for a picturesque backdrop. You can even take a guided tour inside to explore the history and architecture.

- Green Space: Syntagma Square features a lush green area, providing a pleasant spot to relax and people-watch amidst the city's hustle and bustle.

- Shopping and Dining: The square's vicinity offers numerous cafes, restaurants, and shops, making it an excellent place to grab a coffee, a bite to eat, or indulge in some retail therapy.

- Proximity to Attractions: Being centrally located, Syntagma Square is within walking distance of many Athens landmarks, including the historic Plaka neighborhood and the National Garden.

Changing of the Guard Ceremony:

One of the most famous attractions in Syntagma Square is the Changing of the Guard Ceremony that takes place at the Tomb of the Unknown Soldier in front of the Parliament building. This ceremony occurs every hour, 24 times a day, and is a striking display of Greek military tradition. Here's what you should know about it:

- Evzones: The ceremonial guards, known as Evzones, are elite soldiers chosen for their height, physical fitness, and discipline. They wear a distinctive uniform consisting of a pleated skirt (fustanella), white leggings, and red clogs.

- Precise Ritual: The Changing of the Guard is a precise ritual involving synchronized movements, including high kicks and slow, deliberate strides. The Evzones stand motionless for extended periods, a testament to their dedication and endurance.

- Symbolism: The ceremony pays tribute to the Greek soldiers who have sacrificed their lives for their country. The Tomb of the Unknown Soldier is a poignant reminder of the sacrifices made throughout Greece's history.

- Photo Opportunities: Visitors often gather around the guards to witness the ceremony and take photographs. Remember to be respectful and maintain a reasonable distance from the guards.

The synergy of historical significance, architectural beauty, and the mesmerizing Changing of the Guard Ceremony makes Syntagma Square a must-visit destination in Athens. It's a place where tradition and modernity harmoniously coexist, offering travelers a memorable and enriching experience.

Chapter 6. Cultural Experiences

- Greek Cuisine: From Souvlaki to Baklava

No visit to Athens is complete without indulging in the rich and diverse flavors of Greek cuisine. Greek food is a delightful blend of fresh ingredients, Mediterranean influences, and time-honored recipes. Here's a taste of what you can savor in Athens:

1. Souvlaki: This iconic Greek street food is a must-try. Skewers of marinated and grilled meat, often served with pita bread, tomatoes, onions, and a drizzle of tzatziki sauce, make for a delicious and satisfying meal on the go.

2. Moussaka: A beloved Greek dish, moussaka consists of layers of eggplant, minced meat (usually lamb or beef), potatoes, and a creamy béchamel sauce, baked to perfection. It's comfort food at its finest.

3. Greek Salad (Horiatiki): A refreshing and vibrant combination of tomatoes, cucumbers, red onions, Kalamata olives, and feta cheese, drizzled with olive oil and sprinkled with oregano. It's the epitome of Mediterranean freshness.

4. Spanakopita: A delectable pastry filled with spinach, feta cheese, onions, and herbs, all encased in layers of flaky phyllo dough. It's a savory treat that showcases the art of Greek pastry making.

5. Dolmades: Grape leaves stuffed with a mixture of rice, herbs, and sometimes ground meat, these bite-sized delights are typically served as appetizers or meze, often accompanied by a squeeze of lemon.

6. Baklava: Indulge your sweet tooth with baklava, a heavenly dessert made from layers of phyllo dough, chopped nuts (usually walnuts or pistachios), and sweet syrup or honey. Each bite is a perfect balance of crunchy and sweet.

7. Greek Yogurt: Athens is famous for its creamy and thick Greek yogurt. Enjoy it with a drizzle of honey and a sprinkle of nuts for a simple yet divine breakfast or dessert.

8. Ouzo: To complete your culinary experience, try a glass of ouzo, Greece's traditional anise-flavored spirit. It's often served with a small plate of appetizers called meze, creating a delightful combination of flavors.

9. Fresh Seafood: Being a coastal city, Athens offers an abundance of fresh seafood options. From grilled octopus to seafood risotto, you'll find a variety of dishes to satisfy seafood lovers.

10. Greek Coffee: End your meal with a cup of strong and aromatic Greek coffee, typically served in a small, demitasse-like cup. Don't forget to savor the coffee grounds left at the bottom of the cup, which are believed to reveal your fortune.

In Athens, you'll find a plethora of traditional tavernas, cozy cafes, and bustling markets where you can savor these delectable dishes. Whether you're strolling through Plaka, dining in the vibrant Monastiraki Square, or enjoying a meal with a view of the Acropolis, Athens' culinary scene is sure to delight your taste buds and leave you craving more of these unforgettable Greek flavors.

- Traditional Tavernas vs. Modern Gastronomic Ventures

Athens, a city steeped in history and culture, offers a delightful culinary experience that beautifully balances tradition and innovation. When it comes to dining, you'll encounter two distinct but equally enticing options: Traditional Tavernas and Modern

Gastronomic Ventures. Here's a comparison to help you decide where to savor the local flavors:

1. Traditional Tavernas:

Atmosphere: Traditional Tavernas in Athens exude a warm and rustic ambiance. These charming eateries often feature cozy interiors, wooden tables, and a convivial atmosphere, making them perfect for a relaxed meal with family or friends.

Cuisine: Expect hearty, time-honored Greek dishes served with authenticity. You'll find classics like moussaka, souvlaki, tzatziki, and fresh seafood. The emphasis is on simple, locally sourced ingredients prepared with love and tradition.

Experience: Dining at a Traditional Taverna is like stepping back in time. You'll be treated to generous portions of soul-soothing comfort food, accompanied by live Greek music in some establishments. It's a taste of the Greek way of life.

Price: Generally, dining at Traditional Tavernas is budget-friendly, making it an excellent choice for travelers looking for affordable yet delicious meals.

2. Modern Gastronomic Ventures:

Atmosphere: Modern Gastronomic Ventures in Athens offer a contemporary and often upscale dining experience. These restaurants are known for their stylish décor, innovative design, and attention to detail.

Cuisine: Prepare for a culinary adventure. Modern Gastronomic Ventures push the boundaries of Greek cuisine, blending traditional ingredients with cutting-edge techniques. You might encounter fusion dishes, creative tasting menus, and innovative presentations that showcase the chef's artistry.

Experience: Dining at a Modern Gastronomic Venture is a journey for the senses. The focus here is on innovation, aesthetics, and unique flavor combinations. It's an excellent choice for those seeking a gastronomic exploration.

Price: Dining at these ventures can be more expensive compared to traditional tavernas, as you're paying for the creativity and expertise of the chefs.

Choosing the Right Option:

Your choice between Traditional Tavernas and Modern Gastronomic Ventures in Athens ultimately depends on your preferences and the experience you seek. If you're looking to savor authentic Greek flavors in a cozy, nostalgic setting without breaking the bank, opt for a Traditional Taverna. On the other hand, if you're a culinary enthusiast eager to explore inventive Greek cuisine in a contemporary atmosphere, the city's Modern Gastronomic Ventures will delight your taste buds.

In Athens, you don't have to choose just one. Embrace the diversity of the city's dining scene by enjoying both traditional and modern gastronomy, ensuring your culinary journey is as rich and varied as the city itself.

- *Attending a Greek Music and Dance Performance*

A visit to Athens offers not only a journey through history but also a chance to immerse yourself in its vibrant and culturally rich present. One of the most delightful cultural experiences you can have in the Greek capital is attending a traditional Greek music and dance performance. Here's what you need to know to enjoy this captivating aspect of Athenian culture:

1. Finding Performances:

Athens boasts several venues where you can enjoy Greek music and dance performances. Popular choices include the Dora Stratou Dance Theater and the Technopolis in Gazi. Check local event listings or ask your hotel concierge for information on upcoming performances.

2. Types of Performances:

Greek music and dance encompass a wide range of styles, each with its own unique charm. You might encounter:

- Traditional Folk Dances: These are a vibrant display of regional dance traditions from across Greece, each with distinctive costumes and rhythms.

- Rebetiko Music: Often referred to as the "Greek blues," rebetiko music tells stories of love, loss, and resilience. It's a genre deeply rooted in the urban culture of Athens and can be both moving and soulful.

- Contemporary Greek Music: Explore modern Greek music, a fusion of traditional sounds with contemporary influences, often featuring talented local musicians.

3. Dress Appropriately:

While there's no strict dress code for attending these performances, many visitors opt for smart-casual attire. However, you'll also see locals in their everyday clothes, so feel free to wear what makes you comfortable.

4. Arrive Early:

It's a good idea to arrive a bit early to secure good seats, especially if the performance is popular. This also gives you time to soak in the atmosphere and maybe even chat with fellow attendees.

5. Savor Local Delicacies:

Most performance venues offer dining options or nearby tavernas where you can enjoy authentic Greek cuisine. Try classic dishes like moussaka, souvlaki, or Greek salads to complete your cultural experience.

6. Respect the Artists:

During the performance, remember to show your appreciation through applause and cheers. It's customary to express your enjoyment and admiration for the artists.

7. Interact and Learn:

Don't be shy to ask questions or strike up conversations with locals during intermissions. They may be happy to share insights into the music, dance, or cultural significance of what you're witnessing.

8. Take Home Memories:

Capture the moments with photos or videos, but also consider purchasing a traditional Greek musical instrument or a CD of the performers to bring a piece of the experience home with you.

Attending a Greek music and dance performance in Athens is not just a cultural outing; it's a chance to connect with the soul of Greece and its enduring traditions. Whether you're moved by the stirring rhythms or mesmerized by the intricate footwork, this experience will undoubtedly leave an indelible mark on your visit to this remarkable city.

- *Exploring Local Markets: Monastiraki Flea Market*

When you visit Athens, you'll want to immerse yourself in the city's vibrant culture, and one of the best ways to do this is by exploring the Monastiraki Flea Market. This bustling market, nestled in the historic Monastiraki neighborhood, is a treasure trove of sights, sounds, and flavors, offering a truly authentic Athenian experience. Here's what you can expect when you step into this lively bazaar:

1. A Historic Setting:

Monastiraki is known for its historic charm, and the flea market fits right into this picturesque neighborhood. The market's backdrop includes the impressive ruins of Hadrian's Library and the iconic Acropolis, providing a sense of the city's rich history as you shop and stroll.

2. Eclectic Shopping:

The Monastiraki Flea Market is a paradise for shoppers and treasure hunters alike. You'll find a diverse array of items for sale, from antique furniture, vintage clothing, and retro vinyl records to handmade jewelry, local crafts, and souvenirs.

Bargaining is not only accepted but encouraged, so be prepared to haggle for the best deals.

3. Culinary Delights:

As you wander through the market's maze-like streets, you'll encounter numerous street food vendors and small eateries offering mouthwatering Greek dishes. Don't miss the opportunity to savor classic Greek street food like souvlaki, gyros, and loukoumades (Greek doughnuts) while soaking in the lively atmosphere.

4. Cultural Exchange:

The Monastiraki Flea Market is a meeting point for people from all walks of life. You'll likely strike up conversations with both locals and fellow travelers as you browse the stalls. It's a chance to learn about the city from those who call it home and discover hidden gems that may not be in your guidebook.

5. Open-Air Art Gallery:

Art enthusiasts will appreciate the open-air art gallery that often pops up around the market. Local artists display their works, from paintings and sculptures to photography, adding an artistic dimension to your shopping experience.

6. Hours of Operation:

The market is typically open daily, with the busiest days being Sundays when the adjacent Avissynias Square hosts an antique market. It's best to visit in the morning to avoid the crowds and make the most of your shopping expedition.

7. How to Get There:

Monastiraki is a central neighborhood in Athens, and reaching the flea market is easy. It's well-connected by public transportation, including the Athens Metro (Monastiraki Station) and buses. If you're staying in the city center, you can even reach it on foot.

Exploring the Monastiraki Flea Market is a must-do activity for anyone seeking an authentic Athens experience. It's a place where history meets modernity, and where you can find unique souvenirs and memories that will last a lifetime. So, put on your comfortable shoes, bring your appetite, and get ready to dive into the lively atmosphere of this historic Athenian market.

- *Participating in Traditional Workshops (Pottery, Olive Oil)*

One of the most enriching experiences you can have while visiting Athens is to participate in traditional workshops. These workshops offer a unique opportunity to immerse yourself in Greece's rich cultural heritage, learn new skills, and create lasting memories. Two popular traditional workshops in Athens are pottery and olive oil production.

1. Pottery Workshops:

Location: Various locations in Athens, with many workshops located in the historic Plaka neighborhood.

Description: Athens has a deep-rooted tradition of pottery, dating back thousands of years. Participating in a pottery workshop allows you to connect with this ancient craft. Skilled artisans guide you through the entire process,from shaping the clay to painting and glazing your own masterpiece. Whether you're a beginner or an experienced potter, these workshops offer a hands-on experience that is both educational and therapeutic.

Experience: Get your hands dirty as you mold clay into beautiful pottery pieces like bowls, vases, and plates. You'll learn about the history of Greek pottery and the significance of various designs and patterns. Plus, you'll have a unique souvenir to take home, crafted with your own hands.

2. Olive Oil Workshops:

Location: Olive groves and olive oil mills in the countryside surrounding Athens.

Description: Olive oil is at the heart of Greek cuisine and culture. Attending an olive oil workshop takes you to the source of this liquid gold. You'll witness the entire olive oil production process, from harvesting olives to pressing and bottling the oil. Experts share their knowledge about the different olive varieties, extraction methods, and the health benefits of olive oil.

Experience: Roll up your sleeves and participate in the olive harvest (seasonal activity) or learn the art of olive oil tasting. You'll gain a deeper appreciation for this essential ingredient in Mediterranean cuisine. Plus, you can purchase high-quality olive oil to take back home as a flavorful souvenir.

Tips for Participants:

- Reservations: It's advisable to make reservations in advance, especially during peak tourist seasons, to secure your spot in these workshops.

- Dress Appropriately: Wear comfortable clothing that you don't mind getting a little dirty, especially for pottery workshops.

- Ask Questions: Don't hesitate to ask questions and engage with the instructors. They are passionate about their crafts and eager to share their knowledge.

Participating in traditional workshops in Athens is not only a fun and educational experience but also a chance to connect with the local culture in a meaningful way. Whether you choose to shape clay or press olives, you'll create memories that will last a lifetime and gain a deeper understanding of Greece's cultural heritage.

Chapter 7. Outdoor Activities

- *Mount Lycabettus: Hiking and Panoramic Views*

Nestled in the heart of Athens, Mount Lycabettus stands as an iconic natural landmark that offers a delightful blend of outdoor adventure and breathtaking panoramic views. Here, we'll guide you through the experience of hiking this ancient hill and savoring the remarkable vistas it provides.

Hiking Adventure:

Lycabettus, also known as Lykavittos, rises 300 meters (almost 1,000 feet) above sea level, providing an ideal setting for hikers and nature enthusiasts. The journey begins at the base, near the Kolonaki district, and you have two primary options for reaching the summit:

1. Hiking Trail: A well-marked trail winds its way through a lush pine forest, providing shade and serenity along the way. The hike is moderate in difficulty, suitable for both novice and experienced hikers. As you ascend, you'll encounter several viewpoints, offering glimpses of Athens' urban sprawl and the sparkling Aegean Sea.

2. Funicular Railway: For those seeking a more leisurely approach, a funicular railway departs from the base and transports visitors to the top of Mount Lycabettus. This convenient option is particularly appealing for those with mobility issues or limited time.

Panoramic Views:

Upon reaching the summit, prepare to be mesmerized by the unparalleled panoramic views of Athens and its surroundings. The sprawling cityscape unfolds before you, with the iconic Acropolis dominating the skyline. As the sun sets, the Athenian lights come to life, casting a magical glow over the city.

Key vantage points include:

- Acropolis View: The most sought-after view from Mount Lycabettus is, undoubtedly, the Acropolis. You'll capture stunning photographs of this ancient citadel against the backdrop of the Aegean Sea.

- 360-Degree Vista: Wander around the summit's circular viewing platform to witness Athens from all angles. On a clear day, you can even spot the Saronic Gulf islands shimmering in the distance.

Dining and Relaxation:

After your hike or railway journey, take a moment to unwind at one of the hilltop restaurants or cafes. Sip on a refreshing beverage or savor Greek cuisine while absorbing the beauty of the city below. It's an ideal spot for a romantic dinner or a relaxed lunch with family and friends.

Practical Tips:

- Wear comfortable walking shoes and bring water, especially if you plan to hike.
- Check the opening hours of the funicular railway if you opt for this mode of transportation.
- Sunset is an ideal time to visit for the most dramatic views, but it can get crowded, so arrive early to secure a good vantage point.

Mount Lycabettus is not just a hill; it's an experience. It encapsulates the essence of Athens, blending nature, history, and stunning vistas into one unforgettable adventure. Whether you're a nature lover, a history buff, or a photography enthusiast, this iconic Athenian landmark promises an enriching and visually captivating journey.

- *Athens Riviera: Beaches and Seaside Promenades*

The Athens Riviera, stretching along the southern coast of the Greek capital, is a sun-kissed paradise offering a delightful blend of stunning beaches and charming seaside promenades. Here's a glimpse into what this coastal wonderland has to offer in this Athens travel guide:

1. Beaches:

a. Glyfada Beach: This popular beach in the upscale suburb of Glyfada is known for its golden sands and clear waters. It's a favorite spot for locals and visitors alike, offering a vibrant beach scene with numerous beach bars and water sports activities.

b. Vouliagmeni Beach: Nestled in the heart of Vouliagmeni, this beach is renowned for its natural beauty. Surrounded by rocky cliffs and lush greenery, it provides a tranquil escape from the city's hustle and bustle.

c. Varkiza Beach: Varkiza is a family-friendly beach destination with shallow waters, making it ideal for swimming and water sports. Alongside the beach, you'll find a picturesque marina, seafood restaurants, and cafés.

d. Astir Beach: Located in the upscale suburb of Vouliagmeni, Astir Beach is a luxurious escape with crystal-clear waters, comfortable sunbeds, and impeccable service. It's a great place to indulge in a day of relaxation.

2. Seaside Promenades:

a. Athens Riviera Promenade: Stroll along the scenic Athens Riviera Promenade, which stretches for approximately 5 miles (8 kilometers). This charming coastal walkway connects many of the Riviera's beaches and offers breathtaking views of the Saronic Gulf. It's perfect for a leisurely walk, jog, or bike ride.

b. Flisvos Marina: Enjoy a leisurely walk around Flisvos Marina, a bustling waterfront area in the neighborhood of Palaio Faliro. It's not only a marina but also a hub for dining, shopping, and entertainment.

c. Glyfada Promenade: Glyfada boasts a lively promenade lined with palm trees, offering a great place for shopping, dining, or simply taking in the sea breeze. You'll find an array of boutiques, cafés, and restaurants with a Mediterranean flair.

3. Waterfront Dining:

The Athens Riviera is a gastronomic paradise with many waterfront restaurants and tavernas. Sample fresh seafood dishes, traditional Greek cuisine, or international fare while enjoying panoramic sea views.

4. Nightlife:

As the sun sets, the Athens Riviera comes alive with beach clubs and bars that offer a vibrant nightlife scene. Dance under the stars or enjoy cocktails by the sea at venues like Bolivar Beach Bar and Island Club.

Whether you seek relaxation on pristine beaches, a leisurely seaside stroll, or lively entertainment by the water's edge, the Athens Riviera has something for every traveler. It's a picturesque destination that beautifully complements the rich history and culture of Athens, making it a must-visit during your stay in this ancient city.

- *National Gardens: Relaxation Amidst Nature*

Amidst the bustling streets and ancient ruins of Athens, there lies an oasis of tranquility and greenery—the National Gardens. This lush and expansive park, tucked away in the heart of the city, provides both locals and travelers with a serene escape from the urban hustle and bustle.

Location:
The National Gardens, known as "Ethnikos Kipos" in Greek, are centrally located just a stone's throw away from the Greek Parliament building, Syntagma Square, and the bustling Ermou Street. Their prime location makes them easily accessible and a perfect respite from sightseeing.

History:
Originally commissioned by Queen Amalia in the 19th century, the gardens were designed by renowned German landscaper Friedrich von Gärtner. They were initially part of the Royal Palace, serving as the private royal gardens. Today, they are open to the public and offer a glimpse into Athens' regal past.

Features:

The National Gardens encompass 38 acres of meticulously landscaped greenery. As you explore, you'll encounter a delightful array of features:

1. Exotic Flora: The gardens are home to a diverse collection of plants, trees, and flowers from around the world. Stroll among palm trees, cypresses, and vibrant bougainvillea, and discover peaceful corners adorned with fragrant roses and lilies.

2. Majestic Cypress Avenue: A picturesque alley lined with tall, centuries-old cypress trees creates an enchanting pathway, evoking a sense of timeless elegance.

3. Duck Pond: A charming pond inhabited by ducks and turtles adds to the serene ambiance. You can feed the ducks or simply sit by the water's edge and enjoy the natural surroundings.

4. Children's Playground: If you're traveling with kids, you'll find a well-equipped playground to keep the little ones entertained.

5. Zappeion Hall: Within the gardens, you'll find the neoclassical Zappeion Hall, a historic building that hosts cultural events and exhibitions.

6. Botanical Museum: A hidden gem within the gardens is the Botanical Museum, showcasing a diverse range of plant specimens and educational exhibits.

Relaxation and Recreation:
Whether you're seeking a quiet moment of reflection, a leisurely picnic, or a peaceful stroll, the National Gardens provide the ideal setting. Locals often visit for exercise, yoga, or simply to read a book in the shade of a tree.

Practical Information:
- Opening Hours: The gardens are typically open from early morning until sunset. Check for any seasonal variations in opening hours.
- Admission: Entrance to the National Gardens is free, making it an accessible and budget-friendly attraction.

When exploring Athens, be sure to reserve some time to immerse yourself in the natural beauty and serenity of the National Gardens. It's a hidden gem that offers a refreshing contrast to the city's ancient landmarks, providing a well-deserved moment of relaxation amidst nature.

- *Filopappos Hill: Picnics and Sunset Views*

When exploring the vibrant city of Athens, there's one destination that combines history, natural beauty, and breathtaking views into a single experience - Filopappos Hill. This ancient hill, also known as Philopappou Hill, is not only a historical treasure but also a perfect spot for picnics and witnessing mesmerizing sunset views.

Historical Significance
Named after Gaius Julius Antiochus Epiphanes Philopappos, a prominent Roman benefactor of Athens in the 2nd century AD, Filopappos Hill boasts historical remnants that transport visitors back in time. As you ascend the hill, you'll come across the Philopappos Monument, a striking marble mausoleum built in honor of Philopappos. The monument's intricate architecture and the hill's association with ancient Greece make it a must-visit for history enthusiasts.

Picnic Paradise
One of the most appealing aspects of Filopappos Hill is its suitability for picnics. Athenians and tourists alike flock to its grassy slopes to savor moments of tranquility amid nature's embrace. With its lush greenery and ample shade from pine

and olive trees, this hill is an idyllic setting for enjoying a leisurely meal with friends and family.

Sunset Spectacle
While Filopappos Hill is a delightful picnic destination during the day, it truly shines as the sun begins its descent. The panoramic views of Athens from the hill's summit are nothing short of awe-inspiring. As the day turns into evening, the cityscape transforms into a mesmerizing sea of lights. It's an ideal spot for couples seeking a romantic backdrop for their evening, photographers capturing the city's beauty, or simply anyone who wants to witness a breathtaking sunset.

Hiking and Exploration
Beyond picnics and sunset views, Filopappos Hill also offers a network of hiking trails. Visitors can embark on a gentle hike through the hill's pathways, exploring the diverse flora and fauna that call this natural reserve home. The hike culminates with a visit to the summit, where you can enjoy the expansive vistas that stretch from the Acropolis to the Saronic Gulf.

Practical Information
Filopappos Hill is easily accessible from central Athens and the Acropolis area, making it a

convenient addition to your Athens itinerary. Remember to bring a picnic basket with your favorite Greek delicacies, a blanket, and, if you're planning to stay for the sunset, a flashlight for the descent. Comfortable footwear is advisable if you intend to hike the trails.

In conclusion, Filopappos Hill encapsulates the essence of Athens - a city where history meets natural beauty. Whether you're seeking a leisurely picnic spot, a romantic sunset setting, or an opportunity to connect with Athens' rich heritage, this hill is a must-visit destination for travelers seeking a unique and unforgettable experience in the Greek capital.

Chapter 8. Entertainment and Nightlife

- *Rooftop Bars with Awe-Inspiring Cityscapes*

When exploring the vibrant city of Athens, one of the most unforgettable experiences is sipping a refreshing cocktail while gazing out at the breathtaking cityscape from a rooftop bar. Athens is a city steeped in history, and its juxtaposition with modernity is best appreciated from these elevated vantage points. Here, we've compiled a list of rooftop bars that offer awe-inspiring views of the ancient city.

1. A for Athens
Located in the heart of Monastiraki Square, the A for Athens rooftop bar provides an unobstructed view of the iconic Acropolis. As the sun sets over the Parthenon, this rooftop transforms into a magical place to enjoy cocktails and small bites while immersing yourself in Athens' history.

2. 360 Degrees
True to its name, 360 Degrees offers panoramic views of Athens from its rooftop perch in Monastiraki. You'll be captivated by the sweeping vistas that encompass the Acropolis, Mount Lycabettus, and the Aegean Sea. This stylish bar is

perfect for romantic evenings and photography enthusiasts.

3. Galaxy Bar at Hilton Athens
Perched atop the Hilton Athens, the Galaxy Bar combines luxury with stunning views. As you enjoy a signature cocktail or a glass of fine wine, you'll be treated to a postcard-worthy scene of the city below, including the Acropolis and the Saronic Gulf.

4. Couleur Locale
Nestled in the lively Psiri district, Couleur Locale offers a more relaxed and bohemian atmosphere. With its eclectic decor and captivating city views, it's a great place to unwind with friends. The colorful rooftops of Athens stretch out before you, creating a captivating backdrop.

5. The Zillers Athens Boutique Hotel
Located near Monastiraki, The Zillers rooftop bar is known for its vintage charm and views that extend from the Acropolis to the city's urban landscape. Sip on creative cocktails and watch as the ancient and modern facets of Athens harmonize beneath the stars.

6. Point α Bar

Set atop the Herodion Hotel, Point α Bar provides an intimate setting with up-close views of the Acropolis. This gem offers a tranquil escape from the bustling city streets, making it an ideal spot for a romantic rendezvous.

7. St. George Lycabettus
For a slightly different perspective, head to the St. George Lycabettus rooftop bar. Perched on Mount Lycabettus, it offers a bird's-eye view of Athens and the glittering Aegean Sea. This vantage point is especially enchanting at sunset when the city begins to light up.

Whether you're seeking a romantic evening, a place to unwind with friends, or simply a breathtaking view of Athens, these rooftop bars are essential stops on your Athens adventure. Each one offers a unique perspective on this ancient city, reminding you that Athens is a place where history and contemporary charm seamlessly coexist.

- *Plaka's Cozy Cafes and Live Music Venues*

Plaka, nestled at the base of the Acropolis in Athens, is a charming neighborhood known for its cozy cafes and vibrant live music scene. When exploring Athens, a visit to Plaka is a must for those seeking an authentic Greek experience.

Cozy Cafes:
Plaka is dotted with quaint cafes that beckon you to sit, relax, and soak in the ambiance. These cafes are often nestled among the narrow cobblestone streets, offering a perfect escape from the bustling city. Here, you can savor a traditional Greek coffee or indulge in a variety of pastries while taking in the picturesque surroundings. Many cafes also provide outdoor seating, allowing you to enjoy the pleasant Mediterranean climate as you people-watch or simply unwind.

Live Music Venues:
Plaka truly comes alive in the evening, thanks to its vibrant live music scene. Several venues in the area host talented musicians, covering a wide range of genres from traditional Greek music to contemporary sounds. You'll find intimate bars and tavernas where local bands and solo artists perform, creating an atmosphere that's both lively and authentic. Don't be surprised if you're encouraged to join in the dancing or clapping – Greek music has a way of getting everyone involved!

Two notable venues in Plaka include "Taverna Plaka" and "Dipylon." Taverna Plaka offers a taste of traditional Greek music and dance, with live performances that make you feel like a part of a lively celebration. At Dipylon, you can enjoy a more modern musical experience, often featuring jazz, blues, and world music acts.

Whether you're in the mood for a relaxing afternoon coffee or a night filled with live music and dancing, Plaka in Athens has something for every traveler. Its cozy cafes and vibrant music venues are a testament to the city's rich cultural heritage and its commitment to providing unforgettable experiences for visitors. So, make sure to include Plaka in your Athens travel itinerary, and immerse yourself in the enchanting melodies and warm hospitality of this historic neighborhood.

- *Exploring the Gazi District: Clubs and Parties*

When it comes to nightlife in Athens, the Gazi District stands out as the city's ultimate party destination. Located just a stone's throw away from the historical center, Gazi is a vibrant neighborhood known for its electrifying energy, trendy clubs, and pulsating nightlife. In this section of the Athens travel guide, we'll take you on a journey through the heart of Gazi, where the night comes alive, and the music never stops.

The Gazi Experience:
Gazi's transformation into a nightlife hub is nothing short of remarkable. What was once an industrial area filled with gasworks has blossomed into a thriving hotspot for partygoers. The district has managed to retain some of its industrial charm, adding a unique atmosphere to the clubbing experience.

1. Technopolis Complex:
At the epicenter of Gazi's nightlife is the Technopolis Complex. This former gasworks compound has been repurposed into a cultural and entertainment center. It's home to some of the most iconic clubs and bars in Athens. The complex itself is an architectural marvel with its towering chimneys and industrial aesthetics.

2. Gazi's Eclectic Music Scene:
The music scene in Gazi is incredibly diverse, catering to all tastes. Whether you're into techno, house, hip-hop, or even live jazz, you'll find a venue that suits your musical preferences. Popular clubs like "The Hall" and "Six D.O.G.S" often host world-renowned DJs, while more intimate venues

like "Jazz Point" offer a relaxed environment for live music enthusiasts.

3. Open-Air Parties:
One of the unique aspects of Gazi's nightlife is the prevalence of open-air parties during the warm summer months. Rooftop bars and terraces come alive with music and dancing as locals and tourists alike enjoy the pleasant Mediterranean evenings.

4. Late-Night Eateries:
After dancing the night away, you'll inevitably work up an appetite. Gazi has you covered with a plethora of late-night eateries serving delicious Greek street food. Try some souvlaki or gyro to refuel before heading back to the dance floor.

5. Dress Code and Entrance Fees:
Most clubs in Gazi have a relaxed dress code, but it's a good idea to dress stylishly. Entrance fees vary depending on the club and the event, so it's advisable to check ahead and possibly make reservations, especially for popular DJ nights.

6. Safety and Transportation:
Gazi is generally a safe area, but like any nightlife district, it's important to stay aware of your surroundings. Use reputable transportation options

or consider walking back to your accommodation if it's nearby.

Gazi District is Athens' nightlife mecca, where the spirit of celebration never wanes. Whether you're looking for an unforgettable night out dancing to world-class DJs or a cozy spot to enjoy live music, Gazi has it all. So, put on your dancing shoes and immerse yourself in the electrifying rhythms and vibrant atmosphere of this iconic Athenian neighborhood. Your night in Gazi is bound to be an unforgettable experience.

- Open-Air Cinemas: A Unique Movie-Watching Experience

Athens, the ancient and vibrant capital of Greece, offers visitors a multitude of cultural experiences, and among them is the unique and enchanting world of open-air cinemas. Nestled amidst the historic and picturesque neighborhoods of this city, open-air cinemas provide an unforgettable way to enjoy films while immersing yourself in the local culture.

The Atmosphere:
Picture this: a warm summer evening under a starlit Athenian sky, a gentle breeze rustling through the trees, and the aroma of Greek cuisine

wafting through the air. Open-air cinemas in Athens are celebrated for their magical ambiance. These venues are often located in beautifully landscaped gardens, historic courtyards, or on rooftop terraces, creating an atmosphere that seamlessly blends nature, history, and cinematic artistry.

The Experience:
The experience of watching a movie in one of Athens' open-air cinemas is unlike any other. The seating arrangements range from comfy deck chairs to cozy sofas and even traditional Greek lounging cushions. The film is usually projected onto a large screen, ensuring everyone has a perfect view, and the sound is broadcast through quality audio systems.

A Culinary Delight:
What sets Athens' open-air cinemas apart is their culinary offerings. Many of these venues have on-site restaurants or snack bars that serve delicious Greek cuisine. You can savor local delicacies like souvlaki, moussaka, or enjoy a refreshing Greek salad while watching your chosen film. Pair this with a glass of ouzo or a cold beer, and you have a delightful culinary experience to complement your movie.

Cultural Immersion:
These open-air cinemas also provide an opportunity to connect with the local culture. You'll often find a diverse crowd of locals and tourists alike, creating a welcoming and communal atmosphere. It's a chance to enjoy a movie in a unique setting while also experiencing the warmth and hospitality for which the Greeks are famous.

Film Selection:
The selection of films screened in open-air cinemas in Athens is impressive, catering to a wide range of tastes. You can enjoy anything from the latest Hollywood blockbusters to classic Greek and international films. Some venues even host themed film nights or showcase independent and art-house cinema.

Practical Tips:
- Check the schedule in advance, as many open-air cinemas operate from late spring to early autumn.
- Bring a light jacket or shawl as it can get cool at night.
- Arrive a bit early to secure a good seat and take in the ambiance.

- Don't be afraid to ask locals for film recommendations; they may have some hidden gems in mind.

In conclusion, Athens' open-air cinemas offer a captivating blend of film, culture, and culinary delights in a breathtaking setting. It's an experience that combines the allure of cinema with the rich tapestry of Athenian life, making it an absolute must-do for any traveler seeking a unique and memorable evening in this ancient city. So, as the sun sets over Athens, immerse yourself in the magic of open-air cinema and create memories that will last a lifetime.

Chapter 9. Traveling with Kids

- Family-Friendly Attractions: Zoos, Parks, and Museums

Athens, the historic capital of Greece, offers a plethora of family-friendly attractions that cater to travelers of all ages. Among the top choices are zoos, parks, and museums that promise an enriching and entertaining experience for families. Here are some must-visit spots for families exploring Athens:

1. Attica Zoological Park: Located just a short drive from the city center, the Attica Zoological Park is a fantastic destination for animal enthusiasts. This sprawling zoo is home to a diverse range of wildlife, from exotic species to local fauna. Visitors can enjoy close encounters with animals, watch captivating shows, and even participate in educational programs. It's a perfect place for children to learn about the animal kingdom while having fun.

2. National Garden of Athens: Nestled in the heart of Athens, the National Garden offers a serene escape from the bustling city. Families can explore beautifully landscaped gardens, winding paths, and ponds inhabited by ducks and turtles. The garden also features a small zoo with peacocks and other

birds, making it an ideal spot for a leisurely stroll or a relaxing picnic.

3. Museum of Greek Children's Art: This unique museum is dedicated to showcasing the creativity of Greek children. It's an excellent place for young ones to appreciate art and express their own artistic talents through workshops and interactive exhibits. The museum encourages a hands-on approach to learning about Greek culture and history.

4. Goulandris Natural History Museum: Located in the northern suburbs of Athens, this museum is an educational paradise for families interested in the natural world. It houses an extensive collection of fossils, minerals, and taxidermy specimens, making it an excellent place for kids to learn about the Earth's history and biodiversity.

5. Hellenic Children's Museum: Designed exclusively for children, this museum offers a variety of interactive exhibits and hands-on activities that promote learning through play. It's a great place for kids to explore topics like science, technology, and culture while having a blast.

6. Allou! Fun Park: For an adrenaline-packed day of family fun, head to Allou! Fun Park, an amusement

park located in the city. With a wide range of thrilling rides, games, and entertainment options, it's the perfect place for kids and adults alike to enjoy a day of excitement.

7. Benaki Toy Museum: This museum is a delightful journey through the history of toys in Greece. It features an impressive collection of toys from various time periods, providing a nostalgic experience for parents and a captivating one for children.

When planning your family trip to Athens, be sure to include these family-friendly attractions in your itinerary. They offer a perfect blend of education, entertainment, and cultural enrichment, ensuring a memorable experience for the whole family in this ancient and vibrant city.

- Interactive Learning at the Children's Museum

The Children's Museum in Athens offers an enriching experience through its innovative approach to interactive learning. Nestled in the heart of the city, this museum is a must-visit for families exploring Athens.

One of the museum's standout features is its commitment to hands-on engagement. Children of all ages are encouraged to explore, touch, and discover in a dynamic and immersive environment. The museum's exhibits cover a wide range of topics, from ancient Greek history to science and the arts, making learning a thrilling adventure for young minds.

In the "Ancient Athens" section, kids can step back in time and dress up as Athenian citizens, walk through a replica of the ancient Agora, and even try their hand at crafting pottery. This interactive approach not only educates but also ignites a passion for history in young learners.

Science enthusiasts will find the "Science World" exhibit captivating. Through interactive displays and experiments, children can learn about fundamental scientific principles, from gravity to electricity. It's a space where curiosity knows no bounds.

The museum also hosts regular workshops and educational programs, allowing kids to delve deeper into their areas of interest. Whether it's painting, archaeology, or astronomy, there's something for every young explorer to enjoy.

As an added bonus, the Children's Museum in Athens fosters a sense of cultural appreciation. Through art installations, storytelling sessions, and music and dance performances, children can connect with Greece's rich cultural heritage.

In summary, the Children's Museum in Athens is a haven for interactive learning. It engages young minds with its hands-on exhibits, fosters curiosity and creativity, and instills a love for learning that will stay with children long after their visit. Make sure to include this educational gem in your Athens travel itinerary for an unforgettable family experience.

- Kid-Friendly Food Options and Restaurants

Here are the recommendations for kid-friendly food options and restaurants in Athens:

1. Gyros and Souvlaki: These Greek classics are a hit with kids. Whether it's chicken, pork, or beef, gyros and souvlaki are not only delicious but also easy to eat on the go. Many street vendors and local eateries offer these options, making it a convenient choice for families.

2. Pizza: Sometimes, kids just want familiar flavors, and Athens has some excellent pizzerias. These places often have a variety of toppings to please even the pickiest eaters.

3. Greek Meze: Introduce your children to the world of Greek meze, which includes small, shareable dishes like tzatziki, hummus, Greek olives, and stuffed grape leaves. Many restaurants serve meze platters that are perfect for family sharing.

4. Fish and Seafood: If your kids enjoy seafood, Athens is a great place to indulge. The city's coastal location means there's no shortage of seafood restaurants serving fresh catches of the day. Grilled fish or calamari are often kid-friendly options.

5. Child-Friendly Cafes: Athens has a growing number of child-friendly cafes with play areas and menus designed for kids. These cafes provide a relaxing environment for parents while offering snacks and drinks that appeal to children.

6. Ice Cream and Greek Desserts: Treat your kids to traditional Greek desserts like baklava, loukoumades (honey-soaked doughnuts), or a simple scoop of Greek yogurt with honey. Of course, ice cream parlors are abundant too.

Now, let's mention some kid-friendly restaurants in Athens:

1. Ta Karamanlidika tou Fani: This deli-style eatery offers a mix of Greek meze and sandwiches, perfect for sharing with family. It has a cozy atmosphere and a welcoming staff.

2. Hard Rock Cafe Athens: Familiar to many, this international chain offers American-style food with a Greek twist and a lively atmosphere that kids enjoy.

3. Scholarchio: Located near the Acropolis, Scholarchio specializes in Greek comfort food. They have a children's menu and a garden terrace, making it a peaceful spot for families.

4. To Kati Allo: A charming restaurant with a play area for kids, To Kati Allo is a favorite among locals. It offers a mix of Greek and Mediterranean dishes that the whole family can enjoy.

Remember to check restaurant opening hours and make reservations if necessary, especially during peak tourist seasons. Athens is a fantastic destination for family travel, where your children can savor the flavors of Greek cuisine while enjoying the city's historic treasures.

- Tips for Keeping Kids Engaged and Safe

Athens, the historic capital of Greece, is a city filled with ancient wonders, vibrant culture, and exciting experiences for travelers of all ages. When visiting Athens with kids, it's essential to balance exploration with safety and engagement. Here are some tips to help you make the most of your family adventure in this fascinating city:

1. Exploring Ancient Sites Safely: Athens is famous for its ancient ruins like the Acropolis and the Parthenon. While these sites are awe-inspiring, they can also be challenging for young children. Ensure your kids wear comfortable shoes, stay hydrated, and use sunscreen. Consider using a baby carrier or stroller for smaller children to navigate uneven terrain.

2. Interactive Museums: Athens boasts several museums with interactive exhibits that can captivate young minds. The National Archaeological Museum and the Acropolis Museum are excellent choices. They provide engaging displays and educational materials to keep kids

entertained while learning about Greece's rich history.

3. Picnic in the Park: Escape the city's hustle and bustle by spending a relaxing afternoon in one of Athens' parks. The National Garden of Athens is a beautiful place to have a picnic, and it also features a small zoo that children will love. Pack some snacks and enjoy a leisurely day outdoors.

4. Child-Friendly Food Options: Greek cuisine is delicious, and there are plenty of kid-friendly options available. Try traditional dishes like souvlaki or moussaka, which most children enjoy. Many restaurants also offer international cuisine to cater to different tastes.

5. Safety First: Athens is generally a safe city, but it's essential to keep an eye on your children, especially in crowded places. Teach them to be aware of their surroundings and the importance of staying close. Use child safety wristbands with your contact information, just in case.

6. Hands-On Activities: Look for family-friendly tours and workshops that allow your kids to participate actively. Some tour companies offer guided walks designed specifically for families,

providing interesting stories and interactive elements that will make history come alive for your children.

7. Learning Through Play: Visit the Hellenic Children's Museum, where your kids can engage in hands-on activities, interactive exhibits, and creative play. It's a fantastic place for them to learn about Greek culture and history in a fun way.

8. Language and Culture: Encourage your children to learn a few basic Greek words and phrases. Locals appreciate the effort, and it can enhance your family's cultural experience.

9. Transportation: Athens has a reliable public transportation system, including buses and the metro. Consider purchasing an Athens Transport Card to make traveling with kids more convenient. It offers unlimited rides and can save you time and money.

10. Relaxation Time: Don't forget to schedule downtime for your family. Enjoy leisurely walks in picturesque neighborhoods like Plaka, where you can explore quaint shops and cozy cafes while taking a break from sightseeing.

By following these tips, you can create an unforgettable family vacation in Athens, ensuring that your children are engaged, safe, and immersed in the rich history and culture of this incredible city. Athens offers a unique blend of education and adventure that will leave lasting memories for your family.

Chapter 10. Romantic Escapes for Couples

- *Sunset at Cape Sounion: Temple of Poseidon*

One of the most enchanting experiences you can have while visiting Athens is witnessing the breathtaking sunset at Cape Sounion, home to the iconic Temple of Poseidon. Perched majestically on a rocky promontory overlooking the Aegean Sea, this ancient temple is not only a testament to Greece's rich history but also a vantage point for one of nature's most awe-inspiring displays.

As the day draws to a close and the sun descends towards the horizon, visitors gather at Cape Sounion to witness a spectacle that has captured hearts for millennia. The Temple of Poseidon, built in the 5th century BCE, is a magnificent backdrop for this nightly ritual, its Doric columns silhouetted against the colorful canvas of the setting sun.

The warm hues of orange and pink gradually give way to deep purples and blues, casting a tranquil ambiance over the temple and the surrounding landscape. The gentle breeze carries the scent of the sea, adding to the sensory delight of the moment. It's no wonder that poets and travelers throughout history have penned odes to this very spot.

As the sun dips below the horizon, a hushed reverence envelops the crowd. The last sliver of sunlight seemingly ignites the Aegean waters, turning them into a shimmering tapestry of gold. It's a scene that evokes a sense of timelessness and serenity, a reminder of the enduring beauty of the natural world.

Visitors often take their time to explore the temple grounds, soaking in the history and mythology of this place. Poseidon, the god of the sea, was worshipped here, and it's said that sailors of old would come to pay homage, seeking his protection before embarking on perilous journeys.

Today, Cape Sounion stands as a beacon for travelers seeking not only a connection to Greece's ancient past but also a moment of pure transcendence. Whether you're a history enthusiast, a romantic at heart, or simply in search of a serene escape, the sunset at Cape Sounion is an experience that will etch itself into your memory forever.

So, as you plan your trip to Athens, make sure to include Cape Sounion and the Temple of Poseidon in your itinerary. It's a place where the magic of history and nature converge, offering a truly unforgettable encounter with Greece's timeless beauty. Don't miss the chance to witness a sunset that will leave you speechless and inspired, forever carrying the spirit of ancient Greece in your heart.

- *Romantic Strolls in Anafiotika*

Nestled on the northeastern slopes of the Acropolis, Anafiotika is a hidden gem in the heart of Athens that beckons travelers seeking a romantic escape. This charming neighborhood, with its whitewashed houses and labyrinthine streets, transports you to the Greek islands without leaving the city. Here's your guide to experiencing the magic of romantic strolls in Anafiotika.

1. Begin at the Plaka: Start your journey through Anafiotika from the historic Plaka district, known for its vibrant atmosphere. Meander through its colorful alleys and admire the charming shops and tavernas, picking up souvenirs or enjoying a traditional Greek meal along the way.

2. Enter Anafiotika: Ascend the steps leading to Anafiotika, and you'll immediately notice the transformation. The narrow, winding paths, adorned with blooming bougainvillea and quaint gardens, create a picturesque setting for your romantic adventure.

3. Explore the Labyrinth: As you explore Anafiotika, lose yourself in the maze of narrow streets. The architecture, reminiscent of the Cycladic islands, will make you feel like you've been transported to a remote Greek village.

4. Admire the Views: Anafiotika's elevated location offers breathtaking panoramic views of Athens and the Acropolis. Take a moment to savor the scenery and capture memorable photos with your loved one against this iconic backdrop.

5. Visit the Church of Saint George: Make a stop at the Church of Saint George, a small, whitewashed chapel that adds to the area's romantic charm. Its intimate atmosphere is perfect for quiet reflection or a peaceful moment together.

6. Enjoy Sunset: Plan your stroll in the late afternoon to catch the golden hour and witness a stunning sunset over the city. Anafiotika's vantage points provide a front-row seat for this unforgettable spectacle.

7. Savor Local Treats: Along your walk, you'll encounter cozy cafes and traditional bakeries. Indulge in Greek delicacies like baklava or

loukoumades, and don't forget to try a cup of Greek coffee or a glass of ouzo to complete your experience.

8. Embrace the Night: As darkness falls, Anafiotika takes on a romantic glow with lantern-lit streets and the soft hum of conversation. Share a glass of wine at one of the local tavernas, or simply stroll hand in hand under the starlit sky.

Anafiotika, with its enchanting ambiance and timeless beauty, offers the perfect setting for a romantic escapade in Athens. Whether you're a couple seeking to rekindle the flame or simply want to soak in the city's authentic charm, Anafiotika promises an unforgettable experience that will linger in your memories long after your journey ends.

- Couples' Spa and Wellness Retreats

Athens, the historic and vibrant capital of Greece, is not only renowned for its ancient history and archaeological wonders but also offers a perfect setting for couples seeking relaxation, rejuvenation, and quality time together. Amidst the bustling cityscape, you'll discover a haven of tranquility in the form of couples' spa and wellness retreats. These sanctuaries provide the ideal escape from the urban hustle and an opportunity to nourish both body and soul.

1. Electra Metropolis Spa
Located in the heart of Athens, the Electra Metropolis Spa offers a luxurious escape for couples. Step into a world of serenity as you enter this urban oasis. You and your partner can indulge in a range of spa treatments, from soothing massages to revitalizing facials, all designed to promote relaxation and well-being. The spa's rooftop terrace boasts breathtaking views of the Acropolis, providing a romantic backdrop for your wellness journey.

2. Aegle Wellness Center
Nestled in the upscale suburb of Kifisia, the Aegle Wellness Center is a holistic retreat dedicated to rejuvenating the mind, body, and spirit. Couples can explore an array of wellness programs, including yoga and meditation classes, detoxification treatments, and personalized health consultations. The lush green surroundings and serene atmosphere create an ideal environment for couples seeking to reconnect and prioritize their well-being.

3. Hammam Baths

For a unique and culturally immersive experience, visit one of Athens' traditional Hammam baths. These historic establishments offer a glimpse into the city's past while providing couples with an authentic wellness experience. Enjoy a traditional Turkish bath, followed by a soothing massage, all in a beautifully decorated, atmospheric setting.

4. Grecotel Pallas Athena

The Grecotel Pallas Athena, a boutique hotel in the heart of Athens, offers a distinctive spa experience for couples. The "Art 24/7" concept integrates art and wellness seamlessly. The spa features a range of treatments designed to harmonize your body and mind. Afterward, you can savor a romantic dinner at the hotel's rooftop restaurant, with stunning views of the city lights.

5. Island Escape at Lake Vouliagmeni

While not in the heart of Athens, Lake Vouliagmeni is just a short drive from the city center and provides an idyllic escape for couples. The thermal springs at the lake are said to have healing properties, making it an ideal destination for relaxation. You can soak in the warm waters together, surrounded by lush greenery and natural beauty.

Athens' couples' spa and wellness retreats offer a delightful balance to the city's bustling energy. Whether you're looking to unwind with a massage, explore ancient wellness traditions, or simply enjoy each other's company in a serene setting, Athens has a variety of options to help you create lasting memories of relaxation and well-being with your partner.

- Secluded Beaches and Intimate Dining Spots

When one thinks of Athens, images of ancient ruins and bustling city life often come to mind. While the historical treasures of this Greek metropolis are undoubtedly captivating, Athens also offers a quieter, more intimate side that's perfect for travelers seeking tranquility and romance. Here, we unveil some of Athens' best-kept secrets – secluded beaches and intimate dining spots that promise an unforgettable experience.

Secluded Beaches:

1. Astir Beach: Tucked away on the Athens Riviera, Astir Beach boasts crystal-clear waters and a private ambiance. Visitors can relax on sunbeds or indulge in water sports, all while enjoying stunning views of the Saronic Gulf.

2. Vouliagmeni Beach: Located in the coastal suburb of Vouliagmeni, this hidden gem offers natural beauty and calm waters. It's an ideal spot for couples looking to escape the city's hustle and bustle.

3. Legrena Beach: A bit farther from Athens, Legrena Beach is a secluded paradise with its rugged coastline and serene atmosphere. This is where you can truly unwind and soak up the Greek sun.

Intimate Dining Spots:

1. To Kati Allo: Nestled in the charming Plaka neighborhood, To Kati Allo offers traditional Greek cuisine in an intimate setting. The candlelit tables and cozy atmosphere make it perfect for a romantic dinner.

2. Strofi: Perched on the slopes of the Acropolis, Strofi provides not only delicious Greek dishes but also breathtaking views of the ancient citadel. This rooftop restaurant is a prime spot for a memorable evening.

3. Aleria: Located in the heart of Athens, Aleria combines modern Mediterranean flavors with a chic, intimate ambiance. It's a haven for foodies seeking a refined dining experience.

4. Ta Karamanlidika Tou Fani: For a taste of both history and gastronomy, head to this hidden gem in the Psiri district. You'll savor authentic Greek cured meats and cheeses in a rustic, inviting atmosphere.

Athens may be known for its historical riches, but these secluded beaches and intimate dining spots reveal a different side of the city – one that's perfect for couples and travelers seeking romantic escapes. Whether you're lounging on a serene beach or savoring a candlelit dinner, Athens' quieter charms will leave a lasting impression on your heart.

Chapter 11. Day Trips and Excursions

- Delphi: Exploring the Oracle and Ancient Ruins

One of the most captivating day trips you can embark on while staying in Athens is a journey to Delphi. This historic site, nestled on the slopes of Mount Parnassus, is not only a UNESCO World Heritage Site but also a place of immense historical and mythical significance.

Delphi was once considered the center of the world in ancient Greek mythology, and it was here that the Oracle of Delphi resided. Ancient Greeks would pilgrimage to this sacred place seeking wisdom and guidance from the oracle, who was believed to be a conduit to the gods. Today, you can explore the ruins of the Temple of Apollo, where the oracle delivered her cryptic prophecies, and even stand on the sacred ground where ancient leaders sought counsel.

Aside from its mystical aura, Delphi boasts stunning natural beauty. The drive from Athens to Delphi offers breathtaking views of the Greek countryside, with picturesque villages and olive groves dotting the landscape.

Once you arrive in Delphi, the archaeological site itself is a treasure trove of ancient wonders. You can wander through the well-preserved ruins, including the theater, stadium, and treasuries, all while marveling at the ingenuity of ancient Greek engineering and architecture.

The Delphi Museum is also a must-visit, as it houses a remarkable collection of artifacts, sculptures, and art from the site. One of its most famous pieces is the Charioteer of Delphi, a stunning bronze statue that captures the essence of ancient Greek artistry.

As you explore Delphi, take a moment to stand at the precipice overlooking the breathtaking valley below, where the ancient Greeks believed two eagles sent by Zeus met, marking the center of the world. The views alone make the journey worthwhile.

Delphi is an enchanting day trip from Athens that allows you to step back in time and immerse yourself in the mystical and historical wonders of ancient Greece. Whether you're a history enthusiast, a mythology buff, or simply a lover of scenic beauty, Delphi offers an unforgettable excursion that will enrich your Athens travel experience.

- *Hydra and Aegina Islands: Idyllic Getaways*

When exploring the vibrant city of Athens, don't miss the opportunity to escape the bustling urban life and embark on captivating day trips and excursions. Among the many options available, a visit to Hydra and Aegina Islands promises an idyllic getaway that combines rich history, stunning landscapes, and a taste of authentic Greek culture.

Hydra Island: Timeless Charm

Hydra, a gem of the Saronic Gulf, is renowned for its timeless charm and picturesque beauty. This island stands out for its unique character - no motor vehicles are allowed, and transportation is mainly by donkeys or on foot, preserving an old-world atmosphere that is both enchanting and tranquil.

Begin your day by taking a leisurely ferry ride from Athens to Hydra, which takes approximately two hours. Upon arrival, you'll be greeted by Hydra's iconic harbor, lined with vibrant, neoclassical mansions and charming cafes. Take a stroll along the cobblestone streets, admiring the architecture and soaking in the peaceful ambiance.

One of the highlights of Hydra is the Historical Archive-Museum, where you can delve into the island's rich maritime history and artistic heritage. Hydra has also been a muse for many artists and writers, including Leonard Cohen, who resided here, and their influence can still be felt today.

Hydra's beaches, such as Mandraki and Vlychos, offer opportunities for relaxation and swimming in crystal-clear waters. Make sure to savor local cuisine at one of the seaside tavernas, indulging in fresh seafood and traditional Greek dishes.

Aegina Island: History and Flavor

Another captivating destination for a day trip from Athens is Aegina Island, known for its historical significance and culinary delights. Just a short ferry ride away, Aegina is famous for being the first capital of modern Greece.

Start your Aegina adventure by visiting the Temple of Aphaia, an ancient Doric temple with remarkable architecture and panoramic views of the island. Explore the island's charming villages, such as

Aegina Town and Perdika, where you can savor pistachios, Aegina's signature product, and enjoy waterfront dining.

A must-visit on Aegina is the Monastery of Saint Nektarios, a serene and spiritually significant place for Orthodox Christians. The beautiful church and serene surroundings create a sense of tranquility.

Before departing Aegina, don't forget to pick up some local pistachio products, including nuts, sweets, and liqueurs, as souvenirs or delicious treats to enjoy later.

Hydra and Aegina Islands, both easily accessible from Athens, offer unforgettable day trips filled with history, culture, and natural beauty. Whether you're drawn to the serene charm of Hydra or the historical richness of Aegina, these idyllic getaways provide a perfect contrast to the lively pace of Athens, making your visit to Greece truly memorable.

- Corinth and Nemea: Wine Tasting Tours

When visiting Athens, don't miss the opportunity to embark on enchanting day trips and excursions to the nearby regions of Corinth and Nemea. These destinations offer a delightful blend of history, culture, and, of course, exceptional wine tasting experiences.

Corinth, just a short drive from Athens, beckons with its rich historical significance. Explore the ancient ruins of Corinth, including the iconic Temple of Apollo and Acrocorinth fortress, which offer a glimpse into the city's storied past. After immersing yourself in history, it's time to indulge your taste buds.

The Corinth region is renowned for its vineyards, producing some of Greece's finest wines. Join a wine tasting tour and savor the flavors of local varietals, such as Agiorgitiko and Assyrtiko. You'll have the chance to visit charming wineries, meet passionate winemakers, and learn about the winemaking process firsthand. Pair these exquisite wines with traditional Greek meze, and you're in for a memorable culinary experience.

Next, venture further into the picturesque countryside to Nemea, known as the "Land of the Ancient God of Wine." Here, you'll encounter the Nemean Wine Route, a captivating journey through rolling vineyards and idyllic landscapes. Nemea is celebrated for its red wines, especially the robust

Agiorgitiko grape variety. Explore local wineries nestled amidst the hills, and discover the secrets behind their exceptional vintages.

One of the highlights of a Nemea wine tasting tour is the opportunity to participate in a wine and food pairing session. Sample delectable cheeses, olives, and other regional delights that complement the wines perfectly. As you sip and savor, take in the serene beauty of the vineyards and the distant mountains.

Both Corinth and Nemea offer an exquisite blend of history and wine, making them ideal day trip destinations from Athens. Whether you're a history buff or a wine enthusiast (or both), these excursions promise an unforgettable journey into Greece's cultural and culinary treasures. So, raise your glass to a day filled with exploration and enjoyment in the Corinth and Nemea regions.

- *Sounion Peninsula: Beyond the City Limits*

When visiting Athens, the bustling Greek capital, it's essential to explore not only the city's historical treasures but also the captivating destinations that lie just beyond its borders. One such enchanting day trip option is the Sounion Peninsula, a place that takes you on a journey beyond the city limits to discover ancient ruins, stunning coastal landscapes, and a taste of Greece's rich heritage.

The Temple of Poseidon: Your adventure to Sounion Peninsula begins with a scenic drive along the picturesque Athenian Riviera, offering breathtaking views of the Aegean Sea. Your ultimate destination is the Temple of Poseidon, perched majestically atop a rocky promontory. This ancient Doric temple, dedicated to the god of the sea, Poseidon, is an architectural marvel that dates back to the 5th century BC. As you explore its well-preserved ruins, you can't help but feel a deep connection to Greece's mythological past and its seafaring traditions.

Sunset Spectacle: While the Temple of Poseidon is awe-inspiring during the day, it truly comes to life at sunset. Many visitors choose to time their visit to witness the magnificent sight of the sun sinking into the horizon, casting a golden glow over the temple and the surrounding seascape. This experience is nothing short of magical and provides a perfect backdrop for photos and cherished memories.

Lunch by the Sea: Before or after your visit to the temple, don't miss the opportunity to savor authentic Greek cuisine at one of the charming seaside tavernas. Freshly caught seafood, Mediterranean salads, and traditional dishes like moussaka are on the menu. Dining with the sea breeze in your hair and the sound of waves in the background is an experience in itself.

Exploring the Coastal Beauty: The Sounion Peninsula offers more than just ancient ruins. After your temple visit, take some time to explore the coastline. Crystal-clear waters, hidden coves, and small beaches invite you for a refreshing swim or a relaxing sunbathing session. Nature lovers can also go hiking along the coastal trails, providing stunning views of the rugged coastline.

Practical Tips: To make the most of your day trip to Sounion, consider renting a car or joining a guided tour. The drive is approximately an hour from Athens, making it a feasible day excursion. Ensure you have comfortable shoes, sunscreen, and a hat, as you'll be walking and exposed to the sun during your visit.

In conclusion, when visiting Athens, don't limit your exploration to the city's vibrant streets alone.

Embark on a day trip to the Sounion Peninsula, where you can immerse yourself in Greece's ancient history, witness a breathtaking sunset, and enjoy the natural beauty of the Aegean coastline. It's a journey that will not only take you beyond the city limits but also transport you to a realm of myth and wonder, leaving you with memories to cherish for a lifetime.

Chapter 12. Practical Information

- *Language Basics and Useful Phrases*

When visiting Athens, the capital of Greece, it's always a good idea to learn a few language basics and useful phrases to enhance your travel experience. While many Athenians in tourist areas speak English, making an effort to communicate in Greek can go a long way in showing respect for the local culture. Here are some essential language basics and useful phrases to help you navigate Athens:

Greetings and Polite Expressions:

1. Hello! - Γειά σας! (Yia sas!)
2. Good morning! - Καλημέρα! (Kalimera!)
3. Good evening! - Καλησπέρα! (Kalispera!)
4. Please - Παρακαλώ (Parakalo)
5. Thank you! - Ευχαριστώ! (Efharisto!)
6. Yes - Ναι (Ne)
7. No - Όχι (Ochi)
8. Excuse me - Συγγνώμη (Signomi)
9. I'm sorry - Λυπάμαι (Lipame)

Getting Around:

10. Where is...? - Πού είναι...; (Pou einai...?)

11. How much is this? - Πόσο κοστίζει αυτό; (Poso kostizi afto?)
12. I need a taxi - Χρειάζομαι ένα ταξί (Hriazome ena taxi)
13. Bus station - Στάση λεωφορείου (Stasi leoforeiou)
14. Train station - Σταθμός τρένου (Stathmos trenou)

Dining and Food:

15. Menu - Μενού (Menu)
16. Water - Νερό (Nero)
17. Coffee - Καφές (Kafes)
18. I'm a vegetarian - Είμαι χορτοφάγος (Eimai chortofagos)
19. The check, please - Τον λογαριασμό, παρακαλώ (Ton logariasmo, parakalo)
20. Delicious! - Νόστιμο! (Nostimo!)

Shopping:

21. How much does it cost? - Πόσο κοστίζει; (Poso kostizi?)
22. I'd like to buy this - Θα ήθελα να αγοράσω αυτό (Tha ithela na agoraso afto)
23. Do you accept credit cards? - Δέχεστε πιστωτικές κάρτες; (Dexeste pistotikes kartes?)

Emergencies:

24. Help! - Βοήθεια! (Voithia!)
25. I need a doctor - Χρειάζομαι γιατρό (Hriazome giatro)

Learning these basic Greek phrases will not only help you communicate effectively but also make a positive impression on the locals. Athenians will appreciate your effort to embrace their language and culture while exploring this vibrant and historically rich city. Enjoy your time in Athens!

- Emergency Contacts and Medical Services

When exploring the vibrant streets of Athens, it's essential to be prepared for any unforeseen emergencies. Here's a comprehensive guide to emergency contacts and medical services in the Greek capital to ensure your safety and peace of mind during your visit.

Emergency Services:

1. Emergency Number (General): 112 - In case of any immediate emergency, whether medical, fire, or

police-related, dial 112. This number is a universal emergency contact throughout Europe.

2. Police: For non-emergency police assistance, call 100. The Athens Police are generally responsive and helpful.

3. Fire Department: Dial 199 if you require fire-related assistance.

4. Ambulance: To request an ambulance for medical emergencies, dial 166. Athens has a well-organized ambulance service to provide swift medical attention.

Medical Services:

1. Public Hospitals:
   - Evangelismos General Hospital: Located in the city center, this is one of Athens' most renowned public hospitals.
   - Attikon University General Hospital: Situated in the western part of Athens, it's another reliable option for medical care.

2. Private Hospitals:

- Hygeia Hospital: A prestigious private hospital with a range of medical services and English-speaking staff.
- Iaso General Hospital: Known for its excellent healthcare services, including a dedicated international department.

3. Pharmacies: Pharmacies (or "Φαρμακείο" in Greek) are widespread in Athens. Many stay open late, and there's usually one operating 24/7 in each neighborhood. Look for a green cross sign.

4. Medical Clinics: There are various private medical clinics in Athens, offering a variety of specialized services and English-speaking doctors. Examples include the Athens Medical Group and Euromedica.

Travel Insurance:

Before your trip, consider purchasing comprehensive travel insurance that covers medical emergencies. This will provide financial protection and access to quality healthcare services during your stay in Athens.

Language Barrier:

While many healthcare professionals in Athens speak English, it's a good idea to have key medical phrases and terms translated into Greek, just in case. This can help ensure effective communication during medical emergencies.

Athens is a vibrant and safe city, but it's always wise to be prepared. Knowing the emergency contacts and medical services available will help you enjoy your trip with confidence, knowing that assistance is readily accessible if needed.

- Connectivity: SIM Cards and Internet Access

When exploring the vibrant and historic city of Athens, staying connected is essential for navigating its bustling streets, sharing your travel experiences, and accessing vital information. To ensure seamless connectivity, here's a guide to SIM cards and internet access options in Athens.

1. SIM Cards:

Purchasing a local SIM card is one of the most convenient ways to stay connected while in Athens. Greece has several major mobile network providers, including Cosmote, Vodafone, and Wind. You can easily find their stores and authorized resellers throughout the city. Here's what you need to know about SIM cards in Athens:

- Coverage: Greece boasts excellent mobile coverage in urban areas, including Athens. You can expect a strong signal in most parts of the city, even in popular tourist spots like the Acropolis and Plaka.

- SIM Card Types: Greek SIM cards come in various sizes (standard, micro, and nano), so ensure your device is compatible. Many providers also offer tourist-specific SIM cards with data plans tailored to visitors' needs.

- Data Plans: Choose from a variety of data plans based on your usage, from pay-as-you-go options to monthly prepaid plans. Data packages are affordable and provide you with ample internet access during your stay.

- Registration: Be prepared to provide your passport or identification when purchasing a SIM card, as this is a legal requirement in Greece.

2. Wi-Fi Access:

While Athens offers numerous Wi-Fi hotspots in public places, such as cafes, restaurants, and hotels, relying solely on public Wi-Fi might not guarantee a stable connection. Here are some tips for using Wi-Fi in Athens:

- Cafes and Restaurants: Many cafes and eateries in Athens provide free Wi-Fi access to customers. Enjoy a cup of Greek coffee while catching up with friends and family back home.

- Hotels: Most hotels, from budget to luxury, offer Wi-Fi access to their guests. Confirm this service when booking your accommodation.

- Public Transportation: Some public transportation options, like Athens Metro stations and buses, also offer free Wi-Fi for passengers.

- City Hotspots: Athens Municipality has initiated efforts to provide free Wi-Fi in key public areas, such as squares, parks, and pedestrian zones.

In conclusion, staying connected in Athens is a breeze with the availability of local SIM cards and various Wi-Fi options. Whether you choose to purchase a Greek SIM card for reliable mobile data or utilize Wi-Fi hotspots in the city, you'll have the connectivity you need to make the most of your Athens travel experience. Enjoy exploring this ancient city while staying connected to the digital world.

- *Sustainable Travel Practices and Eco-Friendly Initiatives*

Athens, the historic heart of Greece, is not only known for its rich cultural heritage but is also making strides towards sustainability and eco-friendliness. As you explore this vibrant city, you'll find a growing commitment to preserving the environment and promoting sustainable travel practices. Here are some eco-friendly initiatives you can support during your visit to Athens:

1. Public Transportation: Athens boasts an extensive public transportation system, including buses, trams, and a metro system. Opt for these eco-friendly modes of transportation to reduce your carbon footprint while exploring the city. The metro, in particular, is known for its efficiency and cleanliness.

2. Bike-Friendly City: Athens is becoming increasingly bike-friendly, with dedicated bike lanes and rental services available throughout the city. Consider renting a bike to explore Athens at your own pace while reducing emissions.

3. Green Accommodations: Many hotels and accommodations in Athens are embracing sustainability by implementing energy-saving practices, recycling programs, and water conservation measures. Look for eco-certified hotels and boutique lodgings that prioritize environmental responsibility.

4. Local Cuisine: Support restaurants and eateries that focus on serving locally sourced, organic, and sustainable food. These establishments promote traditional Greek cuisine while reducing the carbon footprint associated with imported ingredients.

5. Waste Reduction: Athens has introduced recycling bins and initiatives to reduce waste. Be sure to separate your trash into recyclables and non-recyclables, and support businesses that minimize single-use plastics.

6. Green Spaces: Athens is home to numerous parks and green spaces, including the National Garden of Athens and Pedion Areos Park. Spend time in these urban oases to reconnect with nature and support the city's green initiatives.

7. Cultural Conservation: By visiting Athens' ancient sites, you're contributing to the

preservation of its cultural heritage. Sustainable tourism practices, such as guided tours and respectful behavior, help protect these historic treasures for future generations.

8. Educational Tours: Consider taking eco-friendly tours that focus on the natural beauty and biodiversity of the region. These tours often promote environmental education and conservation efforts in Athens.

9. Shop Local: Choose to shop at local markets and boutiques, which often feature artisanal, handcrafted products. This not only supports the local economy but also reduces the carbon footprint associated with mass-produced goods.

10. Respect for Nature: Whether you're hiking in the nearby mountains or swimming in the pristine waters of the Aegean Sea, always respect the natural environment. Follow responsible tourism guidelines to ensure these beautiful landscapes remain unspoiled.

As you embark on your journey through Athens, embracing sustainable travel practices and supporting eco-friendly initiatives will not only enhance your experience but also contribute to the long-term well-being of this remarkable city and its natural surroundings. Athens is not just a destination; it's a sustainable travel opportunity waiting to be explored.

Chapter 13. Itineraries for Different Travelers

- *3-Day Athens Adventure for Solo Travelers*

Day 1: Exploring Ancient Athens
- Morning: Start your Athens adventure with a visit to the iconic Acropolis. Witness the majestic Parthenon and take in panoramic views of the city.
- Afternoon: Descend from the Acropolis and explore the Acropolis Museum, housing ancient Greek treasures and artifacts.
- Evening: Stroll through the historic Plaka district. Enjoy traditional Greek cuisine at a taverna while savoring live music and Greek dancing.

Day 2: Modern Athens and Cultural Experiences
- Morning: Discover modern Athens by visiting Syntagma Square. Witness the changing of the guards at the Hellenic Parliament and explore the National Garden.
- Afternoon: Head to the Benaki Museum to immerse yourself in Greek history and culture.
- Evening: Experience the vibrant nightlife in Psiri, a trendy neighborhood filled with bars, clubs, and live music venues.

Day 3: Day Trip to the Saronic Islands

- Morning: Take a ferry to the nearby Saronic Islands, such as Aegina or Hydra, for a day of island hopping.
- Afternoon: Explore the charming villages, beaches, and historical sites on the island of your choice.
- Evening: Return to Athens and indulge in a farewell dinner at a rooftop restaurant with a view of the illuminated Acropolis.

Additional Tips:
- Athens is known for its street food, so don't miss trying souvlaki, gyros, and traditional Greek pastries.
- Purchase a multi-site ticket for archaeological sites to save money on entrance fees.
- Use public transportation, like the Athens Metro, to get around the city easily.
- Embrace the local culture by learning a few Greek phrases to engage with the friendly locals.

This 3-day itinerary offers a taste of both ancient and modern Athens, along with the opportunity to explore the beautiful nearby islands. Solo travelers can immerse themselves in the rich history, culture, and vibrant atmosphere that Athens has to offer. Enjoy your Athens adventure!

- Family-Focused 5-Day Athens Exploration

Day 1: Arrival & Acropolis Welcome
- Morning: Arrive in Athens and check into your family-friendly hotel.
- Afternoon: Begin your Athens adventure with a visit to the Acropolis, where you can explore the Parthenon, Erechtheion, and the Acropolis Museum. Don't forget to take in the panoramic views of the city from this historic site.
- Evening: Enjoy a traditional Greek dinner at a local taverna in the Plaka neighborhood.

Day 2: Ancient Agora & Kid-Friendly Fun
- Morning: Discover the Ancient Agora, an open-air archaeological site where you can see the Temple of Hephaestus and the Stoa of Attalos.
- Afternoon: Head to the National Archaeological Museum to see impressive collections of Greek artifacts, including the Mask of Agamemnon.
- Evening: Spend a fun-filled family evening at the Allou Fun Park, featuring amusement rides and games.

Day 3: Seaside Adventures
- Morning: Take a leisurely stroll along the Athenian Riviera in Glyfada or Vouliagmeni.

- Afternoon: Visit the Athens Planetarium for an educational and entertaining experience.
- Evening: Enjoy a relaxing dinner at a seaside restaurant and savor fresh seafood.

Day 4: Day Trip to Delphi
- Morning: Depart for a day trip to Delphi, a UNESCO World Heritage site. Explore the ancient ruins and the Sanctuary of Apollo.
- Afternoon: Visit the Delphi Archaeological Museum to see artifacts from this historic site.
- Evening: Return to Athens and dine at a local restaurant.

Day 5: Hidden Gems & Farewell
- Morning: Explore the charming Plaka neighborhood and Anafiotika, a picturesque area with white-washed houses.
- Afternoon: Visit the Museum of Greek Children's Art, offering creative activities for kids.
- Evening: End your Athens exploration with a farewell dinner at a rooftop restaurant with stunning views of the Acropolis.

Remember to adapt this itinerary to your family's interests and energy levels. Athens offers a rich blend of history, culture, and modern attractions that cater to travelers of all ages, making it a fantastic destination for a family-focused adventure.

- Romantic Weeklong Retreat in Athens

Day 1: Arrival in the City of Gods
- Arrive in Athens and check into a charming boutique hotel with a view of the Acropolis.
- Enjoy a leisurely evening walk to the Acropolis Hill for a breathtaking sunset view.
- Savor traditional Greek cuisine at a cozy taverna in Plaka, Athens' historic neighborhood.

Day 2: Exploring Ancient Love Stories
- Start your day with a visit to the Acropolis Museum to explore ancient Greek art and history.
- Wander through the ancient ruins of the Acropolis, including the Parthenon.
- Discover the Temple of Hephaestus in the serene Ancient Agora, a hidden gem.
- Evening dinner at a rooftop restaurant with an Acropolis backdrop.

Day 3: A Seaside Escape
- Take a day trip to the picturesque coastal town of Sounion.
- Visit the Temple of Poseidon, perched on a cliff with stunning sea views.

- Relax on the beaches of the Athenian Riviera and enjoy seafood by the shore.
- Return to Athens for a romantic evening stroll in the National Garden.

Day 4: Art and Culture
- Explore the National Archaeological Museum for a glimpse of Greece's history.
- Take a scenic drive to the Mount Lycabettus for panoramic views.
- Enjoy an evening at the Greek National Opera or a classical concert.

Day 5: Island Getaway to Hydra
- Embark on a day trip to the charming island of Hydra, just a short ferry ride away.
- Stroll through car-free streets, admire traditional architecture, and relax on pristine beaches.
- Savor fresh seafood at a seaside tavern and enjoy a tranquil day together.

Day 6: Romantic Ruins and Hidden Gems
- Explore the Roman Agora and Hadrian's Library for a more intimate archaeological experience.
- Discover the charming Anafiotika neighborhood, resembling a Greek island village.
- Visit the Benaki Museum to delve into Greek culture.

- A romantic dinner at a rooftop restaurant in Kolonaki.

Day 7: A Farewell to Athens
- Begin your day with a visit to the charming Plaka neighborhood for souvenir shopping.
- Take a scenic stroll to the charming district of Psiri.
- End your romantic retreat with a farewell dinner in a candlelit garden restaurant.

This weeklong itinerary offers the perfect blend of ancient history, breathtaking views, cultural exploration, and moments of intimacy that will make your romantic retreat in Athens unforgettable.

Chapter 14. Local Insights and Hidden Gems

- Lesser-Known Historical Sites and Monuments

Athens is renowned for its iconic historical sites like the Acropolis and the Parthenon, but the city is also home to several lesser-known gems that offer a unique glimpse into its rich history. Here are some hidden historical sites and monuments worth exploring in Athens:

1. Kerameikos Cemetery:
Nestled northwest of the Acropolis, the Kerameikos Cemetery is an ancient burial ground that dates back to the 12th century BC. It's a serene and lesser-visited site where you can explore well-preserved grave markers, sculptures, and the remnants of the city's defensive walls. The site also houses an informative museum dedicated to its history.

2. Roman Agora:
While the Roman Agora isn't as famous as the Ancient Agora, it's a fascinating site that showcases the Roman influence on Athens. Here, you'll find the impressive Tower of the Winds, a clocktower and weather vane, as well as the Gate of Athena

Archegetis. It's a quieter alternative to the bustling Ancient Agora.

3. The Pnyx:
For history enthusiasts interested in the birthplace of democracy, the Pnyx is a must-visit. This ancient assembly space served as the meeting point for Athenian citizens during the 5th century BC. The rock-cut seating arrangement and podium provide a glimpse into the democratic processes of ancient Athens.

4. Panathenaic Stadium:
Often overshadowed by the Acropolis, the Panathenaic Stadium is a hidden Olympic treasure. This marble stadium hosted the first modern Olympic Games in 1896 and is built on the site of an ancient stadium. Visitors can explore its grandstands, Olympic memorabilia, and even run on the track.

5. Hadrian's Library:
Tucked away in the picturesque Plaka neighborhood, Hadrian's Library is a Roman-era monument built by Emperor Hadrian. It was a center of learning and a library during ancient times. Today, you can admire its Corinthian columns and excavated ruins.

6. Church of Panaghia Kapnikarea:
This charming Byzantine-era church, located in the heart of Athens, is one of the city's oldest surviving churches. Its striking architecture and intricate mosaics are a testament to the city's Byzantine history.

7. Stoa of Attalos:
Situated within the Ancient Agora, the Stoa of Attalos is a meticulously reconstructed colonnade that once housed shops and served as a gathering place. Today, it houses the Museum of the Ancient Agora, displaying artifacts from the site.

While Athens is famous for its marquee historical attractions, exploring these lesser-known sites and monuments can provide a deeper appreciation of the city's layered history and cultural heritage. Don't miss the opportunity to uncover these hidden treasures during your visit to this ancient metropolis.

- Off-the-Beaten-Path Dining and Cafes

When exploring the vibrant city of Athens, it's easy to get caught up in the touristy hotspots. However, if you're looking for a more authentic and local dining experience, consider venturing off the beaten path to discover hidden gems in the city's culinary scene. Here are some lesser-known dining and cafe options that promise to tantalize your taste buds:

1. To Kafeneio: Tucked away in the Plaka neighborhood, To Kafeneio offers a taste of traditional Greek cuisine in a cozy, rustic setting. It's a favorite among locals for its hearty moussaka, grilled meats, and welcoming atmosphere.

2. Kiki de Grece: Located in the Exarchia district, this charming little cafe is a haven for coffee enthusiasts. Sip on expertly brewed Greek coffee and indulge in freshly baked pastries while immersing yourself in the bohemian ambiance of the area.

3. Avocado: If you're in the mood for something different, Avocado is a vegetarian and vegan paradise in the heart of Athens. Their creative dishes and smoothies are not only healthy but also bursting with flavors you won't want to miss.

4. Ta Karamanlidika tou Fani: Experience the essence of Greek charcuterie at this small deli and restaurant. Tucked away near Monastiraki Square, it offers a delightful selection of cured meats,

cheeses, and mezze, all served in an atmospheric, historic setting.

5. Little Kook: While not exactly a hidden gem, Little Kook is a whimsical cafe that's often overlooked by tourists. Step into a fairytale world filled with extravagant decor, delectable desserts, and an atmosphere that transports you to another realm.

6. Kuzina: Located in the vibrant neighborhood of Thisio, Kuzina offers modern Greek cuisine with a twist. Their rooftop terrace provides stunning views of the Acropolis, making it an ideal spot for a romantic dinner or a relaxing lunch.

7. Papadakis: For seafood aficionados, Papadakis is a seafood taverna hidden in the picturesque neighborhood of Plaka. Feast on the freshest catch of the day while enjoying a sea breeze on their charming outdoor terrace.

8. To Perasma: Situated in the historic Anafiotika neighborhood, To Perasma is a cozy restaurant serving Greek and Mediterranean cuisine. Its intimate setting and delicious dishes make it a perfect choice for a romantic dinner.

Exploring these off-the-beaten-path dining and cafe options in Athens will not only introduce you to authentic Greek flavors but also immerse you in the city's rich culture and local life. So, venture beyond the tourist traps and savor the culinary delights that Athens has to offer.

- Neighborhood Festivals and Events Calendar

Athens, the vibrant capital of Greece, isn't just known for its ancient history and iconic landmarks. It's also a city that thrives on culture, community, and celebrations. To truly immerse yourself in the local atmosphere, you'll want to explore the Neighborhood Festivals and Events Calendar in Athens. Here's a glimpse of the colorful tapestry of festivities that make Athens come alive throughout the year:

1. Plaka Festival (March): Kicking off the year in style, the Plaka Festival transforms the historic neighborhood of Plaka into a lively celebration of Greek music, dance, and cuisine. It's a fantastic way to experience the traditional side of Athens.

2. Athens Epidaurus Festival (Summer): This internationally renowned festival spans from June to August, featuring a diverse array of cultural

events. From ancient Greek dramas performed in the ancient theater of Epidaurus to contemporary dance and music performances in Athens, this festival is a cultural extravaganza.

3. Feast of St. Dionysios (October): Celebrated in the vibrant neighborhood of Exarchia, this religious festival combines solemnity with festivity. Expect processions, live music, and a vibrant atmosphere that showcases the local spirit.

4. Christmas in Athens (December): The Christmas season in Athens is magical, with Syntagma Square and Ermou Street lit up in festive lights. Enjoy Christmas markets, ice skating, and the warm, welcoming atmosphere that makes this holiday special.

5. Athens Street Food Festival (Various Dates): Throughout the year, various neighborhoods host street food festivals, where you can savor a wide range of Greek delicacies and international flavors. Keep an eye out for these delectable events.

6. Psiri Nights (Ongoing): Psiri is a neighborhood known for its nightlife. The streets come alive with music, dance, and laughter, especially during

weekends. Explore its tavernas, bars, and clubs for an authentic Athenian night out.

7. National Independence Day (March 25th): Celebrated across the city, this holiday commemorates Greece's independence from the Ottoman Empire. Witness the grand military parade on Panepistimiou Avenue and soak in the patriotic fervor.

8. Greek Orthodox Easter (April/May): Easter in Greece is a deeply religious and festive occasion. Join the locals in their midnight church services, followed by a sumptuous Easter feast with lamb and traditional pastries.

Remember that Athens is a city that loves to celebrate, and you'll often stumble upon impromptu street performances, art exhibitions, and cultural happenings throughout the year. To fully appreciate the local culture and the heart of Athens, keep an eye on the Neighborhood Festivals and Events Calendar, as it's a window into the soul of this enchanting city.

Chapter 15. Packing Tips and Souvenir Ideas

- *Weather-Appropriate Clothing Suggestions*

When visiting Athens, it's important to dress appropriately for the weather, which can vary throughout the year. Here are some clothing suggestions to help you stay comfortable while exploring this historic city:

1. Summer (June to August):
   - Athens can get scorching hot in the summer, with temperatures often exceeding 90°F (32°C). Lightweight and breathable clothing is essential.
   - Opt for loose-fitting, light-colored clothing like cotton shirts, shorts, and sundresses to stay cool.
   - Don't forget sunglasses, a wide-brimmed hat, and sunscreen to protect yourself from the intense sun.

2. Spring (March to May) and Autumn (September to November):
   - These transitional seasons offer pleasant weather, but it can still be warm. Layering is key.
   - Pack a mix of short-sleeved and long-sleeved shirts, along with light jackets or cardigans for cooler evenings.

- Comfortable walking shoes are a must for exploring historical sites like the Acropolis.

3. Winter (December to February):
   - Athens experiences mild winters, but it can get chilly, especially in the evenings.
   - Bring a medium-weight coat, sweaters, and long pants. Layering with scarves and gloves can be useful.
   - While it doesn't often snow, it's a good idea to have waterproof footwear for occasional rain showers.

4. General Tips:
   - Athens is known for its ancient ruins, so comfortable and supportive walking shoes are essential year-round.
   - Don't forget swimwear if you plan to visit the beaches along the Athenian Riviera during the summer months.
   - Modest clothing may be required when visiting religious sites, so have a shawl or cover-up for such occasions.

Remember that Athens has a Mediterranean climate, which means plenty of sunshine throughout the year. Checking the local weather forecast before your trip will help you pack appropriately and make the most of your visit to this incredible city.

- Must-Have Items for Exploring Athens

When exploring Athens, there are several must-have items that will enhance your experience in this historic city. Here's a list of essentials for your Athens adventure:

1. Comfortable Walking Shoes: Athens is a city best explored on foot. Ensure you have comfortable, sturdy shoes for walking the ancient streets and climbing the hills.

2. Sun Protection: Athens enjoys a sunny Mediterranean climate. Pack sunscreen, sunglasses, and a wide-brimmed hat to shield yourself from the sun.

3. Water Bottle: Staying hydrated is crucial, especially during the warm months. Carry a reusable water bottle and refill it at the numerous drinking fountains found around the city.

4. Athens Card or City Pass: Consider purchasing an Athens Card or a city pass, which provides access to multiple attractions, public transportation, and discounts at various restaurants and shops.

5. Pocket Map or Smartphone: A detailed map of Athens or a smartphone with GPS and a maps app will help you navigate the city's labyrinthine streets and find your way to its iconic landmarks.

6. Portable Charger: Keep your devices charged so you can access maps, information, and capture memories through photos and videos.

7. Greek Phrasebook: While many Athenians speak English, learning a few basic Greek phrases can enhance your interactions with locals and make your trip more enjoyable.

8. Backpack or Daypack: A small, comfortable backpack is perfect for carrying your essentials, snacks, and souvenirs as you explore Athens.

9. Museum Pass: Athens is home to world-class museums, including the Acropolis Museum and the National Archaeological Museum. A museum pass can save you time and money.

10. Light Jacket or Shawl: Evenings in Athens can be cooler, especially in the off-season. Pack a light jacket or shawl to stay warm when the temperature drops.

11. Cash and Cards: While credit cards are widely accepted, it's a good idea to have some cash on hand for small purchases, as well as for places that may not accept cards.

12. Travel Adaptor: Greece uses Type C and Type F electrical outlets, so bring a suitable travel adaptor to charge your devices.

13. Camera or Smartphone: Athens is a photographer's dream, so don't forget your camera or smartphone to capture the stunning ancient ruins, picturesque neighborhoods, and vibrant street life.

14. Reusable Shopping Bag: Be eco-friendly and carry a reusable shopping bag for any souvenirs or items you may pick up during your trip.

15. First Aid Kit: A small first aid kit with essentials like bandages, pain relievers, and any personal medications can be a lifesaver in case of minor mishaps.

With these must-have items, you'll be well-prepared to explore Athens and immerse yourself in its rich history, culture, and vibrant atmosphere. Enjoy your journey through this captivating city!

- *Authentic Greek Souvenirs to Bring Home*

When visiting Athens, you'll find a plethora of authentic Greek souvenirs to bring home, each offering a piece of Greece's rich culture and history. Here are some must-have souvenirs to consider:

1. Olive Oil: Greece is renowned for its high-quality olive oil. Look for locally produced olive oils in beautifully designed bottles, perfect for adding a touch of Greek flavor to your dishes back home.

2. Greek Pottery: Athens has a long history of pottery craftsmanship. Choose from intricately painted vases, plates, and ceramic figurines, often featuring ancient Greek motifs.

3. Worry Beads (Komboloi): These strings of beads, used for relaxation and meditation, are a popular Greek souvenir. They come in various materials like wood, glass, or semi-precious stones.

4. Handmade Jewelry: Athens boasts talented artisans who create stunning jewelry pieces. Consider silver or gold jewelry adorned with

symbols of Greek mythology, such as the evil eye or the Greek key pattern.

5. Greek Herbs and Spices: Bring the flavors of Greece home with aromatic herbs like oregano, thyme, and rosemary, or unique Greek spice blends. They're perfect for enhancing your culinary creations.

6. Traditional Greek Clothing: You can find clothing items like embroidered blouses, tunics, and sandals, all reflecting Greece's traditional style. These make for fashionable and comfortable souvenirs.

7. Local Wine and Spirits: Greece produces excellent wines and spirits, including ouzo, raki, and tsipouro. Opt for a bottle of your favorite variety to savor the taste of Greece later.

8. Greek Coffee Sets: A traditional Greek coffee set typically includes a small pot (briki), coffee grounds, and demitasse cups. It's a delightful reminder of the country's coffee culture.

9. Handwoven Textiles: Seek out textiles such as scarves, tablecloths, and rugs, crafted using

traditional weaving techniques and adorned with vibrant patterns.

10. Greek Honey and Delicacies: Greek honey is renowned for its exceptional taste and quality. Pair it with other local delicacies like loukoumi (Greek delight) or pasteli (sesame seed candy).

Remember to shop at local markets, like Monastiraki Flea Market and Plaka, for the most authentic and unique finds. These souvenirs will not only remind you of your time in Athens but also allow you to share a piece of Greece's rich heritage with friends and family back home.

Printed in Poland
by Amazon Fulfillment
Poland Sp. z o.o., Wrocław

33739333R00107